# FROM BASICS TO BINDING

## A COMPLETE GUIDE TO MAKING QUILTS

**Library of Congress**
**Cataloging-in-Publication Data**
Buckley, Karen Kay.
From Basics to Binding: A Complete Guide to Making Quilts/by Karen Kay Buckley
p. cm.
Includes bibliographical references.
ISBN 0-89145-991-X: $16.95
1. Patchwork – Patterns. 2. Appliqué. 3. Patchwork Quilts.
I. Title.
TT835.B78 1992
746.9'7 – dc20  92-8990 CIP

Additional copies of this book may be ordered from:

# American Quilter's Society
P.O. Box 3290
Paducah, KY 42002-3290

@$16.95. Add $1.00 for postage & handling

# FROM BASICS TO BINDING

## A COMPLETE GUIDE TO MAKING QUILTS

By Karen Kay Buckley

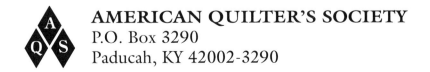

**AMERICAN QUILTER'S SOCIETY**
P.O. Box 3290
Paducah, KY 42002-3290

# Dedication

I would like to dedicate this book to my husband, Joe. I am an extremely fortunate person to have someone like him to help me with my quilting and support my every move. He pushed me to write this book and edited it all along the way. He has spent as much time on this book as I have. I know you would not be reading this now if it was not for him because I would not have worked on the computer, but I would have been quilting instead. I owe him a great deal of thanks. I love you, Joe, and thank you for making another of my dreams come true.

I would also like to dedicate this book to Sue Bousliman. She was my first quilting instructor and gave me a great deal of background from which to build. Thank you, Sue, for teaching me how to quilt and making my life much happier.

# Acknowledgments

I owe four people much thanks. They are my sister, Paula Kissinger, and my friends Ellen Mullen-Hoon, Mary Brevik and Pat McAnally. Thanks to all of you for helping me proof the pages of this book and for your time, support and recommendations.

Much thanks also to the Carlisle Camera Shop, especially Marty. Your time and directions were very helpful.

Thanks to all of my students. Your encouragement was what led me to pursue writing this book. I especially owe thanks to those students who lent me their quilts to be photographed for this book. We could not include all of them because of space limitations, but they are all beautiful. It makes me feel good to see how your love of quilting has developed. Keep quilting!

# Contents

# Introduction

My decision to write this book stemmed from owning a quilt shop and teaching beginning to advanced classes. Having learned much in a very short period of time, my students encouraged me to put my lessons into writing.

Quilts have been around for thousands of years. In its simplest terms, a quilt is three layers: a top layer made of fabric, a middle layer for added warmth and a bottom layer of fabric. All three layers are sewn together with thread, then the edges are bound. The stitches which hold the three layers together are called quilting.

With the proper instruction, everyone is capable of making a quilt. This book is geared for those who are not fortunate enough to have a quilt class in their area or those who wish to supplement a class, as well as for those who are already quilters but want some additional information and patterns.

I believe the best way to get started is to make a sampler project of some size. Much more is learned by making the different blocks in a sampler than by making the same blocks repeatedly. This book will teach you to do patchwork, cutting pieces of fabric into smaller pieces, then sewing them into a new design; and applique, sewing one piece of fabric onto another larger piece of fabric.

The idea of the text is to explain quiltmaking in detail from the beginning – from choosing the designs and the fabric to the final stage of making and applying the binding. Included in this text are several techniques for doing applique, making templates, and piecing, as well as numerous patterns and many exciting quilting ideas. I will attempt to cover as many subjects as possible. The object is for you to try these different techniques, then determine which ones give you the best results.

It is important to keep an open mind. I sometimes have a problem with this myself when I read a technique that has many steps. But when I actually try the technique or combine it with another technique, I often find that my results have improved. Therefore, I have taken a new attitude toward techniques having more steps. If the finished product is better and I am happier with the results, I do not consider the extra steps to be extra work. I simply consider them part of the fun of making the project.

I find quiltmaking to be relaxing. A completed project gives me a sense of satisfaction. I have a rule that helps me reach that satisfaction. My mother always made us finish the things we started. It has rubbed off in my work. I will not allow myself to start a new project until the one I am working on has been completed. I think of the next project and it helps motivate me to finish the one I am working on before starting the next. The result is no unfinished projects. I know this may not be possible for everyone, but try your best to complete each project. It helps keep quiltmaking fun.

Whether you are a beginner first exploring this art or an experienced quiltmaker looking for new techniques and tips, I hope you enjoy working through this book and its projects.

# Section ONE

*A General Introduction to Supplies and Methods*

# SOURCES FOR SUPPLIES

There are a number of supplies you will need for the quilt project you will be making as you work with this book. Purchase all the supplies you need before starting, if possible. This keeps you going through the project without stopping to find supplies.

I cannot suggest strongly enough how important it is to support your local quilt shop. A quilt shop stocks all of the supplies necessary for an excellent finished project.

Discount fabric stores carry some items, but they generally do not have the best quality fabrics, or the specialty items and supplies you will need. Fabric quality is of utmost importance. The better the quality of the fabric, the longer the life expectancy of the quilt. I prefer to pay a little more for supplies because of the amount of time I spend on a project, to ensure that my quilt will be around a long time for my family and descendants to enjoy.

The other factor people sometimes fail to consider when selecting where to purchase their supplies is that salespeople in a quilt shop know a lot about the project you are making. They can offer more assistance in fabric selection and recommend quality supplies.

In case you do not have a quilt shop in your area, there is a list of sources for supplies in the back of this book. These sources are only suggestions. You may find these supplies available elsewhere.

# CHOOSING AND CARING FOR FABRIC

The first and most important item to consider is fabric. Buy only first-quality 100% cotton fabric. It is easier to handle and its life expectancy far exceeds that of polyester and polyester blends.

When choosing fabric for a quilt, consider how the finished project will be used. Decide whether it will cover your bed, hang over your bed, or be used as a throw for the sofa. The colors should match or complement those in the room. Start with a fabric you simply love; then add three or four coordinating fabrics. By restricting yourself to four or five fabrics, the project will be less busy. Keep in mind that a sampler quilt, by its very nature, is busy because of the different blocks. By keeping the number of fabrics to a minimum, your quilt will not become too busy.

Please look through the color portion of this book for ideas that appeal to you. You may decide to use these ideas in your project, but first ask yourself why you like them. Is it because there are two medium-colored fabrics, one dark-colored fabric and one light-colored fabric? Or do you like the color choices because there are no darks, one light and three mediums? Decide what appeals to you and work with it. You can use all prints, all solids, some prints and some solids, large or small prints and even plaids, as long as the colors are coordinated and they make you happy. You are the one who will be looking at this project when it is finished, so you are the one who has to be happy with the colors and fabrics. Do consider including some lights, some mediums and some darks, as the different color shades will add interest to the quilt. My first quilt was monochromatic – the fabrics were all in the same color family, but different tints and shades. It was a safe way for me to start. I still love my first quilt, but today I enjoy working with many different color ideas.

As unpleasant and boring as it sounds (and usually it

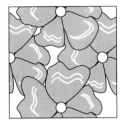

*Figure 1. These fabrics are arranged from light to dark and show nice textures.*

is), you must prewash and iron all of your fabrics. Prewashing is done to ensure that the shrinkage is out of the fabrics and the fabric dyes are colorfast. Staining occurs when the dye of a dark fabric is deposited on a lighter fabric. Sort fabrics for prewashing just as you would regular laundry. Separate lights, mediums and darks to prevent staining. A little hint for reducing fraying: before washing a piece of fabric, clip the four corners with your scissors. By cutting away a small section across the corner, fraying will be prevented (Fig. 2).

Wash all fabrics in warm water with a non-bleaching, basic soap. Of the few good soaps on the market, I prefer Orvus™. It contains no phosphorus and its sulfants are biodegradable. The active ingredient is Sodium Lauryl Sulfate which, because of its basic nature, has proven to be safe for fabrics in that it does not fade them. You will sometimes find this product, labeled "Quilt Soap," in quilt shops. A similar product can also be found, under the name Horvus™, in Agway stores, as it is sometimes used to wash horses. Leather shops are another place I have found it. You only need a small container of this soap. Use approximately one tablespoon for a full load. If you have hard water, use two or more tablespoons.

Another product found to be safe for fabrics is Ensure™, marketed by Mountain Mist®. This soap can be found in many quilt shops, and its bottle gives recommended amounts.

In some supermarkets, you may find another product called Fels Naphtha™. If you decide to use this soap, buy flakes, not the bar.

The next problem to consider is how to best handle dark fabrics. The amount of surface dye used to achieve deep colors can sometimes cause difficulty. The problem is the lack of colorfastness, or release of some of the dyes during washing. When washing dark fabrics, always check the rinse cycle. If the water is clear, the fabrics are safe to use. If the rinse water is slightly discolored, rewash the fabrics again and recheck the rinse water. Some fabrics may continue to bleed. If they do, wash those fabrics with a product called Easy Wash™, as many times as it takes until the rinse cycle is clear. Easy Wash™ can be found in some quilt shops, supermarkets and uniform shops. If you cannot find Easy Wash™, try a home remedy of white vinegar and water. Soaking the

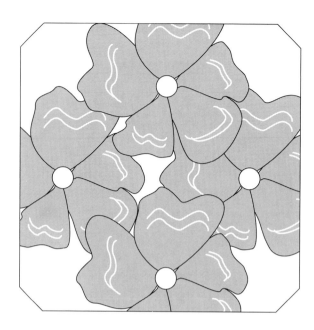

*Figure 2. Corners clipped for prewashing.*

fabric in a mixture of white vinegar and water will sometimes set the color. The Philadelphia College of Textiles recommends that one tablespoon of vinegar be used per gallon of water. They also indicate that salt can be used in place of the vinegar, and in the same amount. I recommend testing a small piece of fabric with the method you plan to use, to make certain it does not fade your fabrics.

After selecting the fabric for the top of your quilt, you must choose fabric for the backing. This fabric can be one of those used in the top, a different fabric or simply, a good-quality muslin. Muslin is a strong, plain fabric in a natural (cream) color, and is very economical. If this is your first project and you have many other supplies to purchase, you may want to use muslin to keep the cost down. Your choice may also depend on how the quilt is to be used. If it is going to hang on the wall, you may take the attitude that no one will see the back; therefore, muslin may be acceptable. On the other hand, if the quilt is to be used as a lap throw or as a bed quilt, you may wish to use a coordinating fabric.

Be sure to buy enough of the fabric before you begin the project. No shop can guarantee being able to obtain more of exactly the same fabric because many manufacturers do a limited printing of their fabric. Even if they do reprint the fabric, the dyes may change so the colors may not match. Because of this, it is always better to have more fabric than not enough. Quilting is great fun, so buy enough fabric from the start to avoid getting frustrated.

Ironing or pressing is my least favorite part of the whole process, but a necessary evil. Pressing means applying heat and pressure to the fabric without sliding the iron across the fabric. It involves setting the iron down, picking it up and setting it down again in order to press the next section. This is done on the seams of piecing and on the top of applique. Ironing means moving the iron across the fabric with a sliding motion. This is done when you are working with a large piece of fabric before any cutting has been done. Iron your fabric using steam and be sure all the wrinkles are removed.

When drying fabrics in the dryer, place a towel in with the fabrics so they will not twist around each other so much. If you pull the fabric out of the dryer when it is slightly damp, it will be easier to iron. Drying the fabric outdoors in a location where it will not be exposed to direct sunlight or indoors using a drying rack is better for the fabric than running it through the dryer. The constant rubbing of fabric against the sides of a dryer can sometimes cause crocking. Crocking is when the fabric shows signs of wear, like the lines that appear on worn blue jeans.

# OTHER SUPPLIES

## SEWING THREAD

You will need one spool of thread to match each of the fabrics you choose. If a shop nearby stocks 100% cotton hand-sewing thread, go for it. However, many shops have a hard time getting 100% cotton so you may have trouble finding it. In that event, cotton-covered polyester can be used; it may twist slightly but it will work fine. Never use 100% polyester thread. It tends to twist and knot during the sewing process.

## INTERFACING

Purchase a ¼ yard of white, medium-weight interfacing for one of the applique techniques. White interfacing will work, no matter what the color of your fabric. CAUTION: Do not buy fusible interfacing.

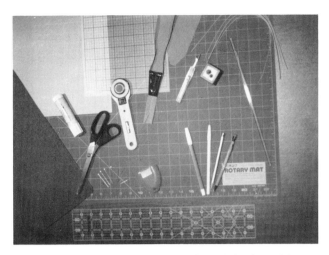

Figure 3. Top, left to right: Clear or frosted plastic, Grid lined plastic, Bias binding maker, Bias press bars, Quilters' Quarter®, Seam ripper, Pencil sharpener; Center Row, left to right: Sandpaper board, Glue stick, Scissors, Rotary cutter; Third Row: Quilting pins, Silk pins, Chalk wheel, Blue washout marker, White chalk pencil, Silver marking pencil, Mechanical pencil; Bottom: Rotary mat or Cutting board, Ruler.

## BIAS BARS

These bars are made of either metal or plastic. You will need one that is ⅜" wide. These bars are used in Lesson 9 to make the bias circle for the wreath. They can also be used for several other applique patterns. I use them for flower stems and some basket handles.

## TEMPLATE MATERIAL

You will need several sheets of plastic to make templates for this project. Some people use paper or cardboard for templates, but the more you mark around the edges of a paper or cardboard template, the smaller the template becomes. With plastic, the template never changes size, remaining accurate. Template plastic comes clear and frosted, with or without grid lines. I prefer to use grid-lined plastic for piecing templates and clear or frosted plastic with no lines for applique templates. For beginners, I recommend clear or frosted plastic because the grid lines can be confusing. Some of my friends who are nurses use old x-ray film.

## RULERS

Not just any ruler will do for quiltmaking. You need a heavy plastic ruler at least ⅛" thick – there are several brands on the market. Test the ruler before you buy it. Place the rulers you are considering on top of some light, medium and dark fabrics to determine which is easiest for you to read. Start with a ruler approximately 3" x 18". Be sure the ¼" mark is easy to read because it will be used more than any of the other lines. Also, choose a ruler with a 45-degree angle marked on it.

## COTTON QUILTING THREAD

Work with 100% cotton quilting thread. Choose the color of quilting thread based on the color of your project. Generally, a quilt is quilted in one color. I usually use off-white quilting thread, because it blends with most fabrics. Therefore, the color of the thread goes unnoticed and you only notice that it is quilted. However, if your fabrics are predominantly white, use white thread. If they are predominantly black, consider quilting using black quilting thread. The idea is for the quilting thread to blend with the project. Quilting thread is much heavier than regular sewing thread because it must hold the three layers of the quilt together. Actual quilting techniques will be discussed in detail later.

## NEEDLES (QUILTING)

There are several different sizes and brands of "betweens," commonly called "quilting" needles. I recommend you start with a size 8, and work into smaller sizes after you have mastered it and feel comfortable. Needles are numbered according to size. The larger the number, the smaller the needle. For example, a size 9 is smaller than a size 8, a size 10 is smaller than a size 9 and so on.

I found that once I felt comfortable with a given size, I was ready to move on to the next smaller size. The smaller the needle, the smaller the stitches, and small stitches are everyone's goal. The only problem with the smaller needle is that the eye of the needle is sometimes hard to thread. There are some companies that make larger-sized eyes. Ask if your quilt shop carries these needles or could order them for you. Size 8 quilting needles will also be used for hand piecing. These needles are shorter and less likely to bend than regular sewing needles. They also give great control, which helps keep stitches smaller.

## APPLIQUE NEEDLES (SHARPS)

You should use a "sharp" to do your applique work.

The best sharps are the English brands. I recommend a size 11 because it is thin and pliable. It makes a small hole and seems to glide through the fabric. The only problem, again, is that the eye is very small and difficult to thread. Cutting the thread at an angle instead of straight across will help in threading it through the eye. Turning the needle and trying the opposite side of the eye may also make a difference.

## THIMBLES

Thimbles come in plastic, leather and metal. If you have never used a thimble, you should start with a long leather thimble. It should fit comfortably on the middle finger of your dominant hand. These thimbles are made of leather on the upper portion and elastic on the bottom inside area. Generally, they are one-size-fits-all and come about two-thirds of the way down your finger. The one disadvantage of the leather thimble is that it wears out. Therefore, if you find a metal thimble that fits your finger and feels comfortable, be sure to buy it immediately.

*Figure 4. From left to right: Paddle thimble; leather one-size-fits-all thimble; tailors' thimble, with no top; and thimble with lip and deep dimples on the top.*

Metal thimbles come in sizes. The larger the number, the larger the thimble. When buying a metal thimble, look for deep dimples or indentations. If the dimples are not deep enough, the needle will roll off the side of the thimble. Depending on how you push with the thimble, there are two areas to look for dimples. I push from the side of the thimble, so the thimble I use has no top and the dimples on the side are very deep. If you push from the top of the thimble, look for a thimble with a lip and deep dimples on the top. About half of the quilters I know push from the top and about half push from the side. Try both methods and select whichever feels the most comfortable to you and produces the best results.

There is also a paddle thimble which you might want to consider. It has very deep dimples. It is held in the palm of the hand, and the round area on the top is used to push. Some people like the comfort of this tool; for example, people with arthritis seem to find this thimble particularly easy to use.

## BATTING

Batting is the inner portion or middle of the quilt, the filler that gives the quilt dimension and adds warmth. There are several different types, brands and thicknesses of batting. For the beginner, a polyester batting that is very thin and easy to quilt through is a good choice. I recommend buying a name-brand, prepackaged batting. With all of the time and effort you will be putting into the project, it is important to know that you are getting a good product that the company will stand behind. Batting purchased from a roll is often very stiff, thick and hard to manage.

When using polyester batting, no space larger than a four-inch square should be left unquilted. This minimum recommended distance between quilting ensures that quilting lines will keep the batting from shifting during laundering.

There are several other battings with their own special uses and considerations. These are explained in a later portion of this book.

## EMBROIDERY THREAD

Embroidery thread is used for one of the applique techniques, the blanket or buttonhole stitch. Check your embroidery thread to make sure the dye is colorfast, just as you did your fabric. An embroidery thread that is not colorfast may bleed into your fabrics when the quilt is washed. You can use Easy Wash™ on embroidery thread if you find that it is not colorfast. Most good craft and fabric shops will supply you with a current list of colors that bleed. Use a six-ply thread and split it into three plies when stitching.

## SEAM RIPPER

This is a metal instrument with a hard plastic handle used to remove incorrect machine sewn stitches.

## SPRAY STARCH

For one of the applique techniques you will need to purchase liquid spray starch. I prefer the brand Spray n' Starch™.

## SANDPAPER

You may find sandpaper an unusual item for a quilting supply list, but it will be very useful. You will need a piece of fine-grained sandpaper. Used with the grain side up under the fabric, it helps to prevent the fabric from shifting while you are marking it, allowing for more accurate lines. There are companies such as Craftistic™ and Quilters Rule™, that sell a thin board with fine-grained sandpaper applied to the top. Sometimes the corners of a piece of sandpaper can start to curl; the board keeps the paper flat at all times so that does not happen.

## GLUE STICK

A glue stick will be used for some of the applique techniques discussed in this book. You will only need a small tube. Be sure the glue stick label states that it is water-soluble. You definitely want the glue to wash from the fabric; you do not want it to be permanent. Keep your glue stick in a cool place because it will melt easily.

## TOOLS FOR MARKING FABRICS

Marking pencils come in many colors. Their use will vary depending on the fabrics you are marking. For most marking, use a simple mechanical pencil with 0.5mm lead. You will always have a fine line, so the marking will be more accurate. If you use a regular pencil, the line gets wider with each stroke. This could cause problems because as the line becomes wider, the fabric pieces become larger. You can keep a pencil sharpener handy and keep the pencil point sharp at all times, but the mechanical pencil will save you much time and will always be accurate.

When marking the back of the fabric for piecing, you need not worry whether it will wash out of the fabric you are using because the markings will never be seen. You simply need to find a pencil that will make lines you can easily see. When marking the back of a dark fabric or a fabric that has a busy design, use either a white pencil or a silver marking pencil. Always keep a pencil sharpener handy, because the lead in these pencils is soft and needs to be sharpened often.

When marking the surface of the fabric, be sure the marker you plan to use will make marks which are visible but not permanent. Test the marker on your fabric, looking for these three qualities: 1. Visibility. You want to be able to see the markings. 2. Ironability. Sometimes the heat from the iron will set the marker in the fabric. I have done this so I know it can happen. It occurred when I marked some quilting lines and when I marked the top of the fabric for applique work. 3. Washability. You want to be sure the markings will, in fact, wash out of the fabric. Test the marker on a small corner of the fabric when the initial washing is done. Mark the area, iron it and then wash the fabric. If the marker disappears, the marker is safe to use.

White chalk-wheels are great markers; the only disadvantage is that their marks will easily brush off the fabric. Therefore, large areas cannot be marked at one time. Mark small areas, quilt these areas, and then move on to the next area to be marked.

Blue washout markers are useful if the project is going to be done in a short period of time. As soon as the project is complete, wash it by hand with one of the soaps recommended in the section on choosing and caring for fabric. I have left markings on fabric for up to three months and had no trouble getting them out. Although labels on the blue markers promise that the markings can be washed out with cold water and a cloth, this is not always the case. The marker's color may migrate into the batting and reappear later on the quilt top. Also, the long-term effect of the chemicals in the marker could harm the fabric. Make sure you thoroughly wash the quilt to ensure that the marker is totally washed out of the project.

You can use a silver marking pencil on the surface of the fabric, but only after it has been tested on the fabric you are using. Silver pencil will wash out of some fabrics and not others. Test it so you will not be upset later because it will not wash out.

One-quarter-inch masking tape can also be used to mark the surface of the fabric. Place the tape along a seam and then quilt down the opposite side of the tape. This is a specialty item and is usually found only in quilt shops. The advantage is that the tape is removed, so there is no washing required. Do not leave the tape on the fabric for long periods of time, as it may leave a sticky residue which is hard to remove.

## PENCIL SHARPENER

There are small sharpeners that you can keep with your sewing supplies so you will not have to look for a place to sharpen your marking pencils while working.

## SCISSORS

Sharp scissors are a necessity. You will also need a pair of paper scissors to cut plastic and paper. Never cut anything but fabric with your good scissors. If you have a good pair of scissors but they are dull, have them sharpened. You will see a world of difference when cutting your fabrics. Sharp scissors allow you to be more accurate. Buy the best you can afford because they will make your work easier and more enjoyable.

## PINS

Believe it or not, there are many different types of pins. You will need long quilting pins with the large ball-heads for hand piecing and for pinning the layers for basting. Although these pins can be used for applique, I prefer silk pins. They are small and thin and are easier to work with on the applique areas. I also prefer silk pins when working at the sewing machine. Your choice of pins will depend on how you plan to approach the project, by hand or by machine.

## BIAS BINDING MAKER

There are different ways to make binding for the edge of the quilt. We will discuss several later in this book. The bias binding maker is a handy tool and should be considered when purchasing your supplies. There are different brands and sizes on the market. I prefer the bias maker distributed by Clover™. The size I use most often is 25mm or one inch. It has a plastic insert and folds the fabric better than some of the other brands. We will discuss binding in detail later.

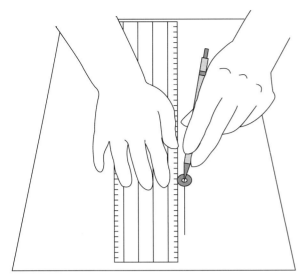

Fig. 5-A

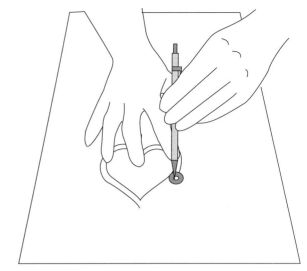

Fig. 5-B

## QUILTERS' QUARTER®

This is a plastic instrument that is one-fourth-inch wide on all four sides. The length varies from about eight to eighteen inches, depending on the company. This tool is easier to use than a ruler when you are marking seam allowance or quilting lines on small areas.

My recommendation is to use either a ruler or a Quilters' Quarter® on the project, but do not interchange them on the same project.

## HALF-INCH WHEEL

This inexpensive tool can be used for numerous things. Called a Wonder Wheel® or a Dream Seamer®, depending on the company, this is a ½" metal washer with a small hole in the middle. If you place a marking pencil in the hole and draw, you will have a perfect ¼" seam allowance. You can use this tool to add a ¼" seam to fabric pieces. Just draw a line down the side of the ruler, then, keeping the ruler at the same place, run the washer down along the edge of the ruler and you have added a perfect ¼" seam (Fig. 5-A). The wheel can also be used to add a ¼" seam allowance to curved portions of applique work. Simply trace around the edge of your template with your marking pencil. Without moving the template, run the wheel around the edge of the template. You have added an accurate ¼" seam allowance (Fig. 5-B).

This handy tool can also be used to mark quilting lines around straight or curved areas. This is more diffi-

cult since you have no edge along which to run the wheel, but it can be effective. It can also be used to echo quilt on curves, a technique used with applique pieces. There is an example of echo quilting in Lesson 14, Folded Sand Dollar Design.

## ROTARY CUTTER AND CUTTING BOARD

These are not inexpensive but are worth every penny, or – should I say – dollar. They are a rotary cutter and a cutting board. The rotary cutter is a hand-held tool with a very sharp round blade at one end. The cutter is used to cut through fabric with a great deal of accuracy. There are several cutters on the market. After trying and working with each one, I prefer the cutter made by Olfa™. Some of the cutters have an angled handle. I found them cumbersome to use, and I found I could not push hard enough to go through all of the layers of fabric.

For the project we are doing, our lattice and borders can be cut with the cutter. A rotary cutter is not necessary for this project because the lattice and border can be cut by hand, but it will save you a tremendous amount of time. The blade of the cutter is sharp, so the safety shield should be closed when the cutter is not in use. Please keep it in a safe place and out of the reach of children. Keeping the safety shield closed is for your benefit and that of anyone else who enters your sewing area. The blade in this cutter is fragile and can easily be nicked. Handle it with care.

Cutting boards are specially made for these cutters.

They are made of a self-healing plastic. After you cut across the board, it heals so the cut does no damage to the board. Do not try to cut on any other surface as it will dull and damage the blade. The blades can be replaced, but they are not cheap. Cutting boards come with or without grid lines. If you are making the investment, make the right one. Buy a board with the grid lines. The gridded board will keep your strips straighter. Use of the cutter and board will be discussed in more detail later.

## HOOP OR FRAME

The last device required is the hoop or frame used for the project. How you approach the project will determine the type used. This book will teach how to do quilt-as-you-go as well as the traditional way of piecing the entire quilt top and then quilting it all at one time. Each method has its advantages which will be explained later in detail.

If you are doing quilt-as-you-go, you will need a square adjustable frame for the blocks. This frame is made of wood and has heavy fabric on the four inner strips of wood (Fig. 6). The frame can be adjusted to the size of the square. The square can be adjusted from approximately 8" to 24". It is handy for quilt-as-you-go and for small wallhangings and pillows.

When selecting a hoop, be sure it is recommended for quilting. Quilting hoops are heavier than those used for embroidery work so that they can hold a lot more fabric. For beginners, I recommend the hoops manufactured by Marie Products™, sometimes called American Heritage™. Hoops come in many different sizes. Start with a 14" size and add other hoops as needed. The screw on the side of the hoop adjusts the tension (Fig. 7). The quilt should be taut and evenly stretched in the hoop when quilting. The hoop will be necessary for the border of the quilt-as-you-go project and can be used for the entire traditional method. With a hoop, you quilt from the center to the outside edges to produce a smooth finished piece.

Lamb Art Press™, under the trade name Q-Snap®, manufactures and distributes PVC frames. The frames are made of high-grade plastic and have plastic clamps to hold the fabric securely in the frame (Fig. 8). I like these for the traditional method. The plastic clamps do

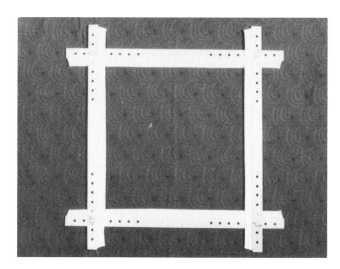

*Figure 6.*

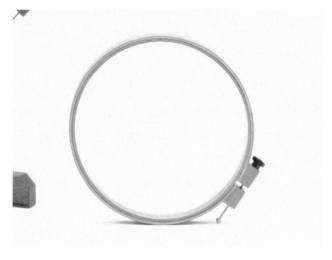

*Figure 7. Photo provided by Norwood Hoops and Frames.*

*Figure 8.*

*Figure 9. Photo provided by Norwood Hoops and Frames.*

not harm the fabric. However, I have found that when the frame is not in use, it is better to remove the clamps from the frame. The clamps can stretch so that they will no longer hold the quilt square tightly in the frame. Q-Snap® frames come in two sizes: 11" x 11" and 17" x 17". The sides of these two squares are interchangeable and will make a rectangular size of 11" x 17", which is nice to use on the border areas. They also come in a floor version which is nice for larger projects, if you are doing the traditional method. The advantage of the floor model is that it can easily be assembled and disassembled. With this type of frame, you quilt from the center to the outside edges, as with the hoop.

Scroll frames are used for the traditional method of quilting, but you need a large area. I have a scroll frame where the width of the quilt is open, but the length is rolled on the wooden rods. The three layers must still be basted, as for all the other hoops and frames discussed to this point. The advantage of this type of frame is that the quilt does not need to be removed from the frame during the quilting process. Therefore, the tension remains the same. You quilt from one side of the quilt over to the opposite side of the quilt for a smoother look when finished (Fig. 9).

The last type of frame is a floor frame. You need a very large area to handle this frame. The older frames are usually made of four wooden boards with sawhorse-type legs. C-clamps are used to tighten and secure the frame. The four wooden slats that form the frame have a strip of heavy fabric along the inside. The backing for the quilt is basted to the four heavy strips of fabric and

then the frame is pulled tight with an even tension. The batting is then centered on top of the backing. Last, the quilt top is centered on top of the batting and basted around all four sides through all layers. No prior basting is required. You quilt from one side to the other and roll the wooden board which is closer to you as you work across the quilt.

My only word of caution on the scroll and floor frames is to be sure the wood is strong enough to support the weight of the quilt you are making. My first scroll frame was made from a softwood and it bowed in the middle because it was not sturdy enough. I have no problems with my new frame made of hardwood.

### FREEZER PAPER

Freezer paper is another unusual item on your supply list. It will be used for some of the applique techniques. Buy the freezer paper that is plastic coated on one side only. This can be found at your local supermarket. It is better to use a brand-name freezer paper, to ensure good quality. I prefer Reynolds®.

### POSTER BOARD

White poster board is the last of the supplies. This is used for an applique technique. Do not use colored poster board. If you cannot find poster board, you may use anything that is about the same weight as poster board – manila folders or the thin cardboard inside shirt packages.

## FABRIC GRAIN

Fabric has a lengthwise grain, a crosswise grain and a bias. These grains are described in relationship to the selvages of the fabric, the edges of the fabric where the threads are tightly woven to finish off the edges. The selvage should never be included in your pieces because there is more shrinkage in the selvage than in the rest of the fabric. Crosswise grain runs from selvage to selvage. There is a little stretch on the crosswise grain. The lengthwise grain runs parallel to the selvages. There is little or no stretch on this grain of the fabric. The bias of the fabric runs on the diagonal and has much stretch. If the grain is not straight in the fabric you have purchased, it can be straightened, but only when the fabric is wet. To straighten it, pull on the bias.

The grain line should run on the outside edge of your units and outside edge of your blocks. Avoid using bias on the outside edge of a block.

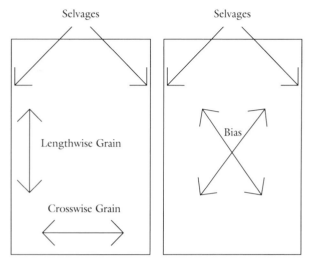

*Figure 10. Fabric grain.*

The only exception to this is directional fabrics which may need to be cut differently for a design purpose. If you are working with a directional fabric like a stripe, be sure to follow the design and not the grain line. For the purpose of quilting it is more important to have the design flow evenly.

In quiltmaking, we simply refer to the grain line. Either crosswise or lengthwise can be used. The arrow on the pattern will indicate where the grain of the fabric should be placed.

## QUILTING: QUILT-AS-YOU-GO VS. TRADITIONAL METHOD

As with any technique, there are pros and cons. The method to use for your first project can either be the quilt-as-you-go method or the traditional method.

In the quilt-as-you-go method, one block is pieced, then immediately quilted. The pre-quilted sections are later joined to create a quilt. The main advantage to this method is the size you work with – it is not as overwhelming as a whole top, and a single block is easier to handle. You will also see from the first block to the last the improvement of your quilting stitches. I always tell my students that their stitches will get smaller with practice. They usually have doubts, but when they stick

with it they find it gets easier and their stitches do get smaller. The results come earlier with this method. Using the traditional method of putting the entire top together and then quilting it all at one time, you don't begin to quilt until the entire top is together.

You can also carry the smaller version with you as you work on the blocks. It is not heavy to handle. Some of my students liked the mobility of the project. They could take it in the car and work while waiting to pick up their children from a sporting practice or game. They could even sit by the pool with it.

The drawback of this method is that there are more seams. This means purchasing a little more lattice and more backing fabric to accommodate these seams. (The lattice is the fabric that separates the blocks. Refer to the section on assembly of the top for a picture of the lattice.) You must also purchase a quilt-as-you-go square frame for the blocks and a hoop for the borders.

The traditional method has its advantages as well. As there are fewer seams on the top and back, you can purchase less of the backing and lattice fabric. Assembly time is also slightly less because there are fewer seams.

The disadvantages of the traditional method are that it is not as mobile, and the quilting can seem overwhelming because it will all need to be done at the same time.

## MAKING TEMPLATES

The method you use to make templates will depend on whether you are hand sewing or machine sewing. Hand and machine sewing will be discussed immediately following this section.

Although previously mentioned, it must be emphasized that working with plastic is better than working with cardboard or paper. Paper products will get smaller as you trace around them, so you will lose your accuracy. Accuracy is the most important part of making templates and marking fabrics.

Here are some different ways to make templates. Try all of them and use the one that gives the best results and is the most accurate. Template patterns will vary in different books, patterns and magazines. Sometimes they will include the sewing lines only, sometimes the cutting lines only and sometimes both the sewing and the cutting lines. Be sure to read the accompanying text before working with the patterns (Fig. 11).

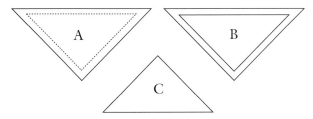

*Figure 11. A: Dotted line is the sewing line; solid line is the cutting line. B: Inside solid line is the sewing line. Outside solid line is the cutting line. C: One solid line usually means sewing line only.*

If you are having a problem with a pattern, the first thing to do is to go back and check your templates. Place your plastic template over the ones in the magazine, book or pattern. If they are correct according to the pattern, then the problem may be that the pattern was printed an incorrect size, in which case you will have to draft your own templates. If you are planning to make a whole quilt of one pattern, it is always a good idea to make one block to confirm that the size is correct and the pieces are accurate. Label all of your templates with a number or letter to correspond with the pattern. Also, be sure to transfer the grain lines from the pattern onto the template. It is also a good idea to put the name of the pattern on the template. This way, if you choose to make the pattern again, you will not need to remake the templates. I place my templates in an envelope and mark the name of the pattern on the envelope.

## METHOD ONE

When making the first template, trace only the sewing lines on the plastic. Place the plastic over the pattern piece. As these lines must be straight and accurate, always use a ruler to draw them. Never try to draw a straight line without one. Use a pencil or a fine-point pen to trace on your plastic. If you use a permanent fine-point marker, you must allow a small amount of time for the ink to dry. There is a black pencil made just to mark on plastic, but it is difficult to sharpen to a fine point and may cause inaccuracy.

After the lines are traced, you need your paper scis-

sors to cut the template. Cut just inside the sewing line you drew. If you cut outside the line, you increase the size of the piece on all sides. When I say just inside, I mean right along the edge of the line you drew. Do not cut too much away or the template will be too small.

The template is then placed on the back of the fabric. This is where the fine-grained sandpaper comes into play. Place the sandpaper on your work area with the rough side facing up. Put the fabric on top of the sandpaper with the wrong side of the fabric facing up. Place the template on the top of the fabric. Trace around all sides of the template with your pencil at an angle. This helps to stop the pencil from skipping on the fabric. Try to draw the line one time only. The more times you have to draw, the greater the chance of inaccuracy.

The next step is to trace the ¼" seams around all sides of the pattern. Use your ruler for this by placing the ¼" marking of the ruler on the lines you just drew, then drawing along the edge of the ruler. This makes accurate seam allowances. You can also use your Wonder Wheel® or your Quilters' Quarter® to add the seam allowance. These lines are your cutting lines. With this method, the lines that are the most important are the sewing lines. If the cutting lines are slightly off, it will not affect the finished piece. This method can be used for hand or machine sewing.

## METHOD TWO

Trace the template, using the cutting lines. Then move to your fabric and draw around the template. Next, using your ruler, draw a ¼" seam allowance on the inside edge of the cutting lines. This, also, is an accurate way of making the template. This method can be used by either hand or machine piecers. With this technique some experienced machine sewers choose not to draw their sewing lines, and use their cutting lines as a guide. You would then sew a ¼" seam with your machine, using the cutting lines as a guide. This will be explained more in the machine sewing section.

## METHOD THREE

The next way to make a template is to trace the sewing lines and the cutting lines on the plastic. Cut on the cutting lines with your paper scissors. With a sharp, pointed instrument, punch a hole at the intersecting points on the sewing lines. You could use an ice pick or the point on a compass to make the holes. Keep the holes small. Do not use a holepunch because the hole gets too big, causing inaccuracy. Punching holes in the plastic will cause protrusions on the back side of the template. Place the plastic with the protrusions against the fabric so they will grip it. With the template on the wrong side of the fabric, trace the cutting lines and mark the dots. Lift the template from the fabric and use your ruler or Quilters' Quarter® to connect the dots. Hand and machine sewers can use this method (see Fig. 12).

### METHOD FOUR

Freezer paper can be used to make templates. Place the freezer paper over the pattern with the paper side up and the coated side down and trace only the sewing lines. Cut the freezer paper template and press it to the back of the fabric with the coated side down. Use a dry iron, no steam. Do not leave the iron on the freezer paper for a long time; it only takes a few seconds. If the paper is not at the exact spot on the fabric you want it to be, it can be pulled up and pressed again. The templates can be used until the coating no longer takes hold. Draw the ¼" seam allowance on all sides and cut the fabric on the cutting line, leaving the freezer paper on the back of the fabric. The freezer paper is left on the fabric and used as a guide for the sewing line, then removed. This method can be used by machine and

hand sewers. If you accidentally sew into the freezer paper template, it cannot be used again with accuracy. You will need to make a new one.

## APPLIQUE

Applique is the process of placing one piece of fabric on top of another and stitching them together. There are numerous ways to do applique. In the following lessons I have explained several different applique techniques. I have found all of these techniques to be successful and I recommend that you try them all. As I mentioned earlier, keep an open mind. Some of these techniques have more steps than others. But, if at the end of the technique your applique is better, the time was well spent. When some of these techniques were explained to me, I made funny faces and said, "Why bother?" Since then I have tried these techniques. Now I know the answer – the finished piece is much nicer.

## PRESSING

Pressing is essential to an accurate finished piece. Finger pressing can sometimes distort seams, so do not finger press. If you do not know what this is, do not worry; you have no bad habit to break. Press the seams with a dry iron. Steam can sometimes stretch and distort the pieces. The seams should be pressed to one side or the other. Never press the seams open as is done in dressmaking. Pressing the seams to one side or the other makes a stronger seam. Seams should be pressed very flat. It is better to lift the iron and place it back

*Figure 12.*

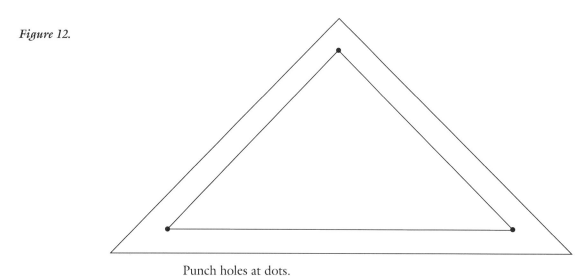

Punch holes at dots.

down on the next section to be pressed rather than slide it across the fabric and the seams. This is especially true for applique because it sits up off the surface of the background fabric. Press from the back first, then flip the block over and press again from the top. It takes time to go to the iron but it is worth every step. Think of it as a form of exercise! The general rule for pressing seams when piecing is to press towards the darker fabric and away from light fabric. This prevents shadowing of the darker fabric through the surface of the light fabric. The general rule is to press the rows so that the seams will butt. For example, if you have a block with four rows, press the seams in rows one and three in one direction and those in rows two and four in the opposite direction. This will allow the seams to butt at the intersections when you join the rows. Also, press the seams away from the area where you plan to quilt. Avoid quilting through seams whenever possible. After the block is finished, use light steam to press the block.

## FIGURING YARDAGE

You will need to measure your bed to determine the amount of fabric required for your quilt. Measure from the top to the bottom of your mattress and from the side to the side of your mattress. Determine how much of a drop or overhang you want off the side and bottom of the bed. Some people have a dust ruffle and like to drop the quilt approximately three inches past the top of the ruffle. Some people have older beds and like to see the wood on the sideboards. It is up to you and your taste. Take the measurement from the top to the bottom and add this to twice the drop measurement. The reason you double the drop is because it needs to drop on both sides.

Using the measurement from side to side, add the drop, times two. This gives you the width you need when it is finished. I add three inches to each of these measurements, as quilting will shrink the size of the quilt approximately three inches in each direction. You must allow for this in the beginning. I am giving you a yardage chart for the quilt-as-you-go method. If you are doing the traditional method, reduce the lattice by ½ yard and the backing by ½ yard (see Fig. 13).

## CUTTING BORDERS

The borders should be cut first to be sure you have

*Figure 13.*

## YARDAGE CHART*

| | Blocks*** | Size of Blocks Only | Finished Size | Lattice**** | Blocks** | Binding | Outer Border | Inner Border | Backing |
|---|---|---|---|---|---|---|---|---|---|
| Wallhanging | 6 (3x2) | 44" x 28" | 52" x 36" | ¾ yd | ½ yd | ½ yd | 1 yd | | 3¼ yds |
| Twin | 15 (3 x 5) | 44" x 70" | 54" x 90" | 1¾ yds | 1 yd | 1 yd | 3 yds | 2½ yds | 7½ yds |
| Double | 20 (4 x 5) | 56" x 70" | 72" x 90" | 2½ yds | 1¼ yds | 1 yd | 3 yds | 2¾ yds | 11 yds |
| Queen | 30 (5 x 6) | 70" x 84" | 90" x 108" | 3 yds | 1½ yds | 1¼ yds | 3¼ yds | 3 yds | 11 yds |
| King | 36 (6 x 6) | 84" x 84" | 108" x 108" | 3½ yds | 1¾ yds | 1½ yds | 3¼ yds | 3¼ yds | 12 yds |

This chart gives approximate yardages; measure your bed for exact yardages.
* For quilt-as-you-go-method. Reduce lattice by ½ yd. and backing by ½ yd. for traditional method.
** Chart includes using four different fabrics in the blocks. Example: If you were doing the wallhanging size project you would purchase ½ yd. of each of your four fabrics.
*** Add an extra row of blocks to bed quilts if tucking under your pillow.
****Lattice measurement is lattice only. It does not include enough for blocks.

the length you need. The yardage requirements you have been given allow for the borders to be cut as one piece.

You are now able to determine how wide you need to make your horizontal and vertical borders. You will figure the hoizontal and vertical borders the same way, using different starting dimensions. You will want to use the same border width on all four sides, so you will need to decide which of the two final measurements you will actually use.

As an example, we'll use a quilt top consisting of 12" blocks, four across and five down:

To calculate the width needed for the borders running across the quilt, begin with the combined dimensions of the blocks across the quilt. In this case that would be 4 blocks x 12" or 48".

Add to that figure the lattice measurements. The lattice is two inches wide for the traditional and for the quilt-as-you-go method, and there are five strips across the quilt so that measurement would be 5 x 2" or 10":

48" + 10" = 58".

Then subtract the amount above from the finished quilt width you desire. If you would like your finished quilt to be 72" wide, the results would be as follows:

72" - 58" = 14".

Then, add three inches to the measurement to allow for the shrinkage of quilting:

14" + 3" = 17".

Since there are two borders, this measurement must be divided by two:

17" ÷ 2 = 8.5".

The ideal borders running the length of the quilt would each be cut 8.5" wide.

To determine the ideal width for the borders running the length of the quilt, begin with the combined dimensions of the blocks down the quilt: 5 blocks x 12" = 60".

Add to that figure the lattice measurements. The lattice is two inches wide for the traditional and for the quilt-as-you-go method, and there are six strips across the quilt so that measurement would be 6 x 2" or 12":

60" + 12" = 72".

Then, subtract the amount above from the finished quilt width you desire. If you would like your finished

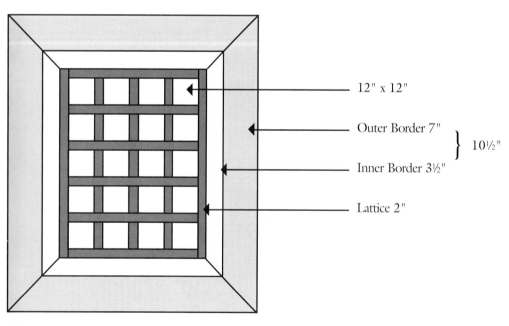

12" x 12"

Outer Border 7"

}

10½"

Inner Border 3½"

Lattice 2"

*Figure 14.*

quilt to be 90" long, the results would be as follows:

90" - 72" = 18".

Then, add three inches to the measurement to allow for the shrinkage of quilting:

18" + 3" = 21".

Since there are two borders, this measurement must be divided by two:

21" ÷ 2 = 10.5"

The ideal borders running the width of the quilt would each be cut 10.5" wide.

You will now need to choose between these two measurements. Generally the larger measurement is used. So in this case instead of using borders 8.5" wide, we would opt for using borders 10.5" wide on each side. With a border this width, you would want both an inner and outer border. The inner border is the one closest to the center. The outer border is generally wider than the inner border.

On this sample I would make my inner border 3½" (cutting the border 4" to include the seam allowance).

I would make the outer border 7" (cutting the border 7½" for the seam allowance) as shown in Fig. 14.

You can mark these borders with a ruler and cut them by hand or with a rotary cutter. Using whichever method you choose, cut the borders first. Cut the length of the fabric required before you start cutting for your blocks. This way you will not have to seam your borders.

You can cut the borders and the lattice with the rotary cutter. This is one of the most accurate time-saving devices ever invented for the quilter. Fold the fabric so you get the length you need. I fold the fabric raw edge to raw edge so the selvages are along the outside edge. Then bring the fold over to the raw edges. Lay the fabric on the cutting board to keep the fabric as flat as possible. It is now four layers thick. Place the fold of the fabric on one of the lines of your grid board. Then line the ruler up with the line on the grid board closest to the selvage edge of the fabric. Place your fingers on the ruler to anchor it and lean on it. Keep your hand firmly on the ruler and use even pressure as you cut.

Start the cutter on the board above or below the fabric, depending on the direction you are cutting and take it to the opposite side and bring it off the fabric. Cut a straight edge on the fabric, being sure to remove the selvage. Do this by cutting along the right side of the ruler if you are right handed, and along the left side if you are left handed. Then move the ruler over to the line which will give you the width you need. Place the cutter at an angle to the board. Push or pull the cutter along the edge of the ruler. The correct way is to push the cutter away from you, but I cannot get enough pressure when I push away, so I cut toward myself. If you are cutting toward yourself, stand away from the table so that you do not cut yourself. Keep the blade of the cutter along the edge of the ruler. Push down on the cutter to enable you to cut through the four layers of fabric. There is a safety shield on the cutter. Some of the shields will open automatically when you push on them and others need to be pulled open. Always keep the shield closed when the cutter is not in use. These blades are very sharp. You do not want to cut yourself or have someone else bump into the blade. You may want to practice on some scraps before cutting into the real thing.

When cutting strips for the lattice or strip piecing projects, fold the fabric selvage to selvage. Then take the fold over to the selvage. The fabric is now four layers thick and the strips cut will be 44"-45" long. This method of folding the fabric differs from the method used when cutting borders, because there you need a longer strip. The way to fold the fabric when cutting borders was explained earlier on this page.

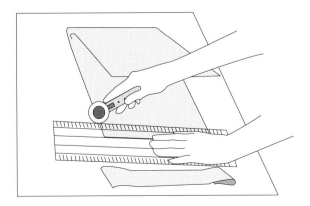

*Figure 15.*

27

# Section Two

## *Lessons*

This section is broken down into lessons, each designed to teach you something different and to give you a new challenge. New techniques and ideas will be explained in each lesson, so if you decide to skip one, please read through it anyway, to help you understand the next. Included at the end of the lessons are several additional patterns that will seem easy after going through the lessons.

The blocks in this book are all 12" x 12" when finished. Unfinished, they should measure 12½" x 12½" from edge to edge. Check each block when you finish it; if it is not the correct size, check your templates and the ¼" seam allowance.

# Lesson ONE

## Triangles, Straight Piecing and Butting Seams

Make a template for the triangle below. Place your plastic over the triangle design and trace the lines using a ruler. These lines must be straight and accurate. Use your paper scissors to cut just inside the lines you have drawn.

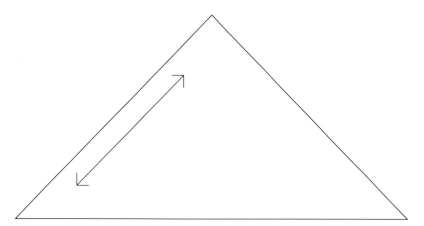

*Figure 1-1.*

### MARKING THE FABRIC

You will trace your triangle on the wrong side of the fabric. Place sandpaper, with the rough side up, under your fabric so the fabric does not slip and the lines will be more accurate. Use a mechanical pencil, if possible; the thin lines will be more accurate. It does not matter whether these lines will wash out or not since they are on the back, but do not use ink. Ink can bleed through to the surface of the fabric.

Position the triangle template so that two sides are on grain lines; the base of the triangle will fall on the bias. Then trace along the three sides. When tracing, pull the pencil at an angle along the side of the template. These lines will be your sewing lines. With the ¼" mark on your ruler or with the use of your Quilters' Quarter®, add a ¼" seam to all sides of the triangle. These lines will be your cutting lines. Fig. 1-2 shows the best way to draw your triangles on the back of the fabric with very little waste.

Cut eight triangles from four different fabrics. You will have a total of 32 triangles for your first block. The blocks in Figure 1-3 are all good blocks to use for the first lesson. You can do all or one of them. How many you do will depend on the size of the project you are going to make.

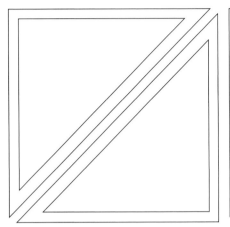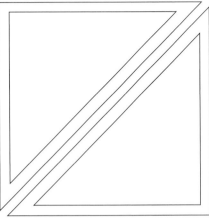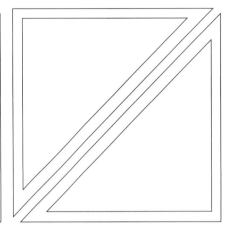

*Figure 1-2*

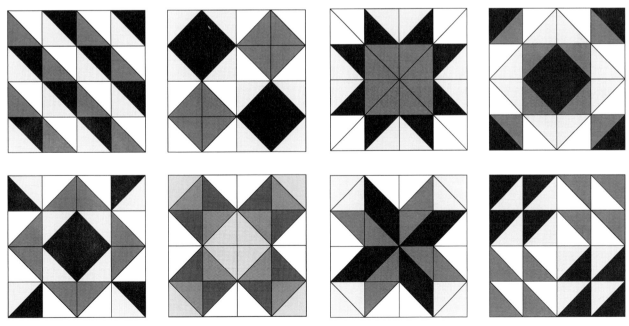

*Figure 1-3.*

## SEWING THE TRIANGLES TOGETHER

Choose one of the patterns in Figure 1-3 or make a design of your own which uses triangles. Lay your fabric triangles out to create all of the designs and choose the one that you like the best. It is fun to see how different the blocks look, even though you are using the same fabric triangles in each. If you are doing a bigger project, you can make several of these blocks in the same quilt because they will look very different.

After you choose a design, find a flat surface for your working area. Lay the triangles out in the design you have chosen. You will be sewing the triangle blocks in units and then rows. Refer to the picture below.

Try to always sew in units and rows. If you get into this habit, you will find that you make few, if any, mistakes sewing pieces in the wrong direction (Fig. 1-4).

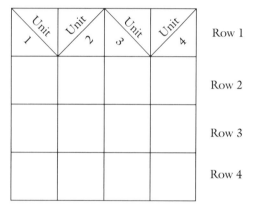

*Figure 1-4.*

You must now choose whether you will hand piece or machine piece. Piecing by hand is a good choice for those who have never sewn or have done little sewing. I recommend hand sewing for those just beginning. It is more relaxing, more accurate – and less frustrating because fewer seams have to be ripped.

Place the two pieces to be sewn together front-to-front and pin on the line. Pin the ends first, then the lines in between usually fall into place. However, always put pins through the lines to be safe. The lines on the piece behind should be lined up with the lines facing you (Fig. 1-5). Check each time you insert a pin.

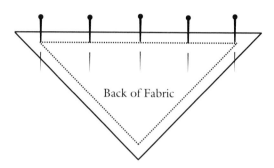

*Figure 1-5.*

Hand piecing is done with a single strand of thread that matches the fabric. Thread your needle and tie a knot at one end. I use size 8 quilting needles. The best stitch to use is a running stitch. Try to take two to three stitches on your needle at a time (Fig. 1-6). Keep the stitches small and even. You should be sewing 8 to 10 stitches to the inch.

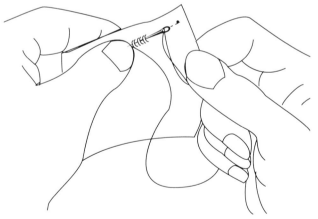

*Figure 1-6.*

Sew from ¼" seam to ¼" seam, not edge-to-edge of the fabric (Fig. 1-7).

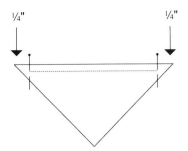

*Figure 1-7.*

Sew past the pins on the line and then remove them. This helps to keep the fabric from shifting and keeps the seams even. Check the back occasionally to make sure you are stitching exactly on the marked lines. Make a knot at the end and clip the thread. Press the seams from the back, then from the front. Make sure the seams are flat. If you are sewing triangles, diamonds or anything with tails, clip the tails (Fig. 1-8).

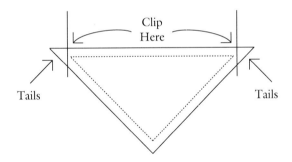

*Figure 1-8.*

If you are dealing with butting seams when joining units, lift the seams and sew through the base of the seams. The seams are too thick to keep your stitches small and even. Pinch the seam allowances up towards yourself and stitch just under the seam's stitched line (Fig. 1-9).

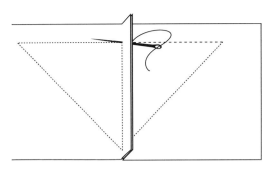

*Figure 1-9.*

Intersections such as these can be weak spots for hand sewers. Therefore, do a backstitch at all of these intersections. A backstitch is simply going back one stitch and then continuing sewing. It acts like a knot and helps to secure the seam. I prefer to take the backstitch before I enter the intersection. Some people prefer to do it after crossing the seam. The choice is yours, but be sure to take the backstitch. You can take the backstitch on both sides if you choose.

If your choice is machine sewing, make sure your machine is in good working order. Set the stitch length at 12 stitches to the inch. Again, you will be working with the fabric with right sides together. You will sew from the raw edge of the fabric to the raw edge (Fig. 1-10).

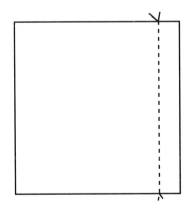

*Figure 1-10*

When starting, I recommend pinning pieces together to ensure the edges are in line. Many machine sewers use one color of sewing thread (such as off-white or light gray) for the entire project. Change threads if there is a drastic change in the colors of fabric. Mark your ¼" seam lines until you are able to judge and handle the ¼" seam on your sewing machine. One way of sewing with a ¼" seam is to run a piece of masking tape along the ¼" seam line on the machine so you will always be sewing with an accurate ¼" seam. The edge of your presser foot may be an accurate ¼" or it may not. Check your presser foot before you start. To check the ¼" seam, use your plastic ruler and place it under your presser foot. Drop the foot and the needle, lining it up with the ¼" marking on the ruler. Bring the needle down to the ruler without pushing the needle into the ruler. If you need to make a guide with tape, you can run one piece of tape or you can stack the tape several pieces deep. The latter makes a small lip along which to run the fabric (Fig. 1-11).

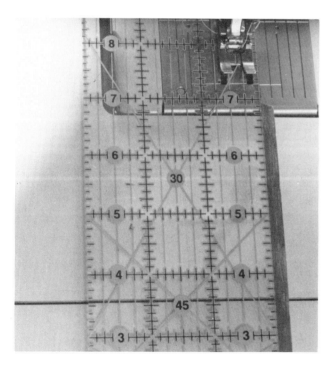

*Figure 1-11.*

By running the fabric along the tape, you will not have to watch the foot on the machine all of the time (Fig. 1-12).

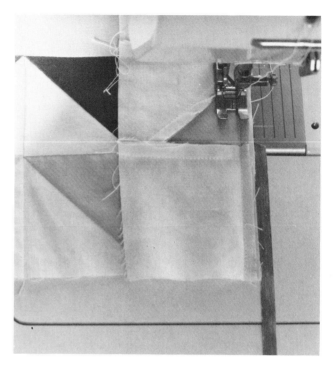

*Figure 1-12*

The correct way to machine sew is to remove the pins as you come to them. Do not sew over your pins as this may cause damage to your machine. If you must sew over pins, do so very slowly and carefully. You do not need to backstitch at the end of the pieces. By sewing to the end of the fabric, you have reinforced the seam.

Unlike in hand sewing, when machine stitching butting seams, you will sew over them instead of through them (Fig. 1-13).

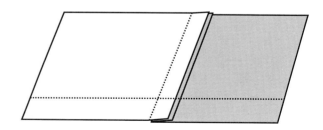

*Figure 1-13*

The direction for pressing the seams in machine sewing is important. Seams in adjoining rows should be pressed in opposite directions to reduce bulk and to make them easier to match. The best advice I can give is to use sewing lines for your first project so your seams will be accurate. Also, clip the threads as you go.

You should change the needle in your sewing machine after ten hours of sewing. The needle dulls with use and can cause problems.

Whether using hand or machine sewing there are some basic rules: do as much straight line sewing as possible; do not do set-ins unless absolutely necessary. Set-ins are when you have to sew a piece into an angle, as shown in Fig. 1-14.

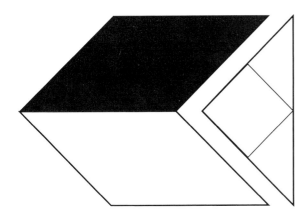

*Figure 1-14*

Sharp, accurate points are important to the look of the finished piece. If you are hand sewing, pin the points and sew through the points. If you are machine sewing, pin an X across the points. Put one pin in through the point. Do not secure the pin. It is used only to position the point. Use two pins, one on each side, to anchor the point. Place these two pins in an X through the fabric. Remove the center positioning pin and sew across the top where the seam lines intersect (Fig. 1-15).

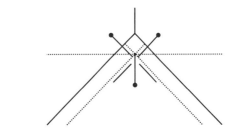

*Figure 1-15.*

## SEWING THE BLOCK TOGETHER

Sew triangles in units and rows. Remember to sew the units and press those seams to one side before sewing the rows together. Press the seams toward the darker fabric. Press the seams for rows one and three in one direction and the seams for rows two and four in the opposite direction. Sew row one to two, two to three and three to four. Press those seams either up or down. See Fig. 1-16 for a full example.

Break a block down into units and rows when possible. Always sew in the same order, from top to bottom and from left to right with the units. That way you will make fewer mistakes and never sew the wrong units or the wrong rows together.

This block can be broken down and pieced as follows:

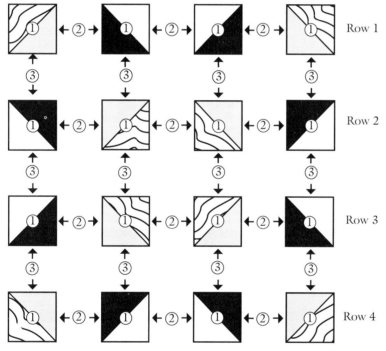

Row 1

Row 2

Row 3

Row 4

Step 1: Sew units.

Step 2: Sew units together.

Step 3: Sew rows together.

*Figure 1-16.*

## LATTICE

If you are using the quilt-as-you-go method, you are now ready to add the lattice. If you are using the traditional method, please move to Lesson 2.

Cut two strips 1½" wide and 12½" long and sew these to the sides of your block. Cut two strips 1½" wide and 14½" long. Sew these to the top and bottom of the block. These measurements include the seam allowances. If you are hand sewing, mark the ¼" seam allowance as a sewing guide. It is easier to mark these lines before the fabric is cut. After the lattice is cut, the pieces are too small for you to accurately mark the sewing lines. Press the seams away from the center. The lattice will be the same size and color for all of the blocks in the project (Fig. 1-17).

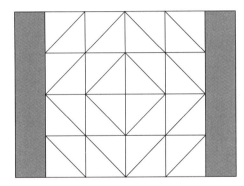

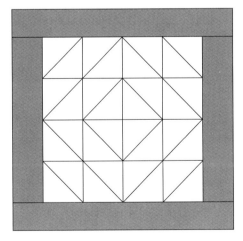

*Figure 1-17.*

## BACKING AND BATTING

Cut one 16" x 16" square of batting and one of backing fabric. Make a sandwich using the backing on the bottom, batting in the middle and the pieced block on the top. Pin these three layers together. The batting and backing will be larger than the top. This is just a reminder so you do not think you have done something wrong. These layers should be assembled on a flat surface to ensure everything stays flat and even. Check the back for puckers. The diagram below shows how and where to place the pins (Fig. 1-18).

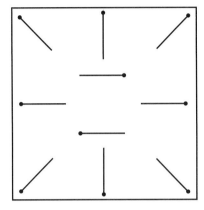

*Figure 1-18.*

## BASTING THE BLOCK

Baste with a double strand of sewing thread, using a large running stitch in a color not in your block so the stitches will be easy to see when you are removing them. Baste as shown in the diagram below (Fig. 1-19). The outside basting stitch should be approximately ½" from the edge. You can now remove the pins.

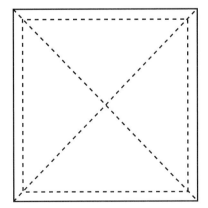

*Figure 1-19.*

## ADJUSTING THE WOODEN FRAME TO SIZE

Follow the directions on the package to assemble the frame.

If you are using a Marie Products™ square frame (Figure 1-20), place the screws and nuts in the eighth hole from the outside edge. After you have it squared, tighten all four screws. Pin one side of the block, through all three layers, to the fabric portion of the frame. It will take five or six pins on each side. Pin the opposite side of the block to the frame, then pin the other two sides. Be sure the block is tight in the frame. If your block is loose, it will be difficult to handle. You can leave it pinned to the frame or you can baste the block into the fabric portion of the frame.

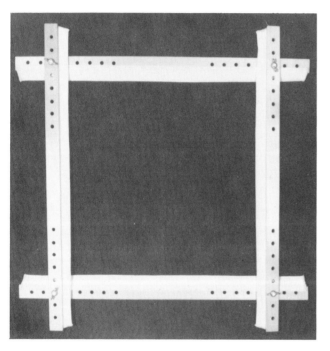

*Figure 1-20.*

## MARKING QUILTING LINES

The quilting design can be marked before or after the piece is basted. When you mark your lines will depend on the marker you are using. For example, if you are using chalk, it is better to wait until after the piece is basted so it does not brush off of the fabric before you are ready to quilt. If you are using a silver or white pencil, you may find it easier to mark the lines before the piece is basted. The ¼" tape or the blue marker can be used either before or after basting.

The quilting design is your choice. There are some suggestions in this book, but feel free to create your own. Children's coloring books and cookie cutters are just two other sources of ideas for quilting designs. They are simple yet interesting. The only area of caution is to be sure to do enough quilting to keep the batting from shifting when the quilt is washed and handled. The amount of quilting needed to hold the batting in place is discussed in the section on differences in batting.

It is always easier to quilt a design that does not cross over any seams. The thickness of the seams makes it difficult to keep the quilting stitches as small as in other areas. Sometimes, though, this cannot be avoided.

If you are quilting very close to the seam lines, it is not necessary to mark any lines. The stitches will hardly show because they become buried in the seams. This style of quilting is commonly called quilting "in the ditch."

## QUILTING IDEAS

Mark your quilting lines referring to previous sections on marking tools. Fig. 1-21 shows some possible designs for the block used as a sample in this lesson.

You are now ready to quilt this block. Refer to the section on quilting which begins on page 98.

After your block is quilted, remove it from the frame and remove the basting stitches.

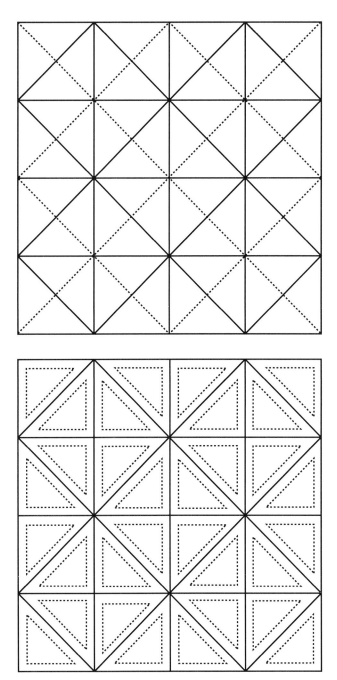

*Figure 1-21.*

# Lesson Two

## *Grandmother's Flower Garden: Applique with Glue and Set-Ins*

For the Grandmother's Flower Garden block you have a choice of hexagon sizes. The first size is a 1" hexagon. If you choose this size, you will need one hexagon for the center, six hexagons for the petals and 12 hexagons for the leaves. See the diagram and the template for this in Fig. 2-1.

The second choice is the 1½" hexagon (Fig. 2-2). With this, you will need one center hexagon and six hexagons for the petals.

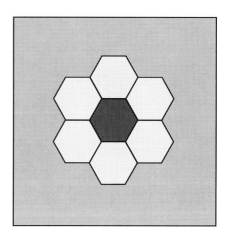

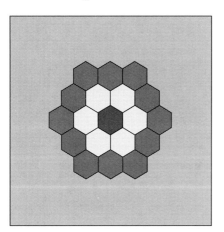

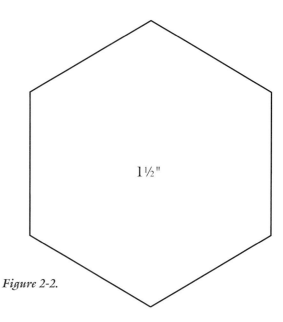

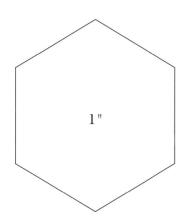

1"

*Figure 2-1.*

1½"

*Figure 2-2.*

Select the size hexagon you want to use for your block, make a template using the pattern on page 40, and cut the number of fabric pieces you need (adding seam allowances as in Lesson 1). Sew the petal section in units of two hexagons each, as shown below in Fig. 2-3. Press the seams in a circular fashion so they are all going in the same direction. Connect the units to the center hexagon. Press these seams away from the center.

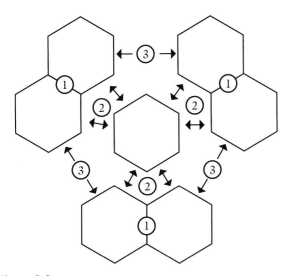

*Figure 2-3.*

Backstitch at every intersection. If you are using the 1" hexagon, you will need to now add the leaves. These can be added one at a time or in units of two, as the petals were added.

## USING THIS BLOCK AS A SIGNATURE BLOCK

All of your projects should be signed or labeled. If you are making a larger project, this block makes a good signature block. If you are making a wallhanging, it may be better to sign the back. If you are signing on the back, the signature is generally placed on the bottom corner. What's fun about the sampler quilt is that you can hide the signature on one of the blocks. The center hexagon in this block can be signed.

When signing, there are several methods. You can do it with embroidery thread using a satin stitch or a backstitch. You can also cross stitch the signature. Your quilt can also be signed with an indelible marker. These markers come in a range of colors, so you should be able to find one to complement the fabrics used in your

project. Test the marker to be sure it will not run.

If you are signing on the back, there are some preprinted labels available. I recommend using Pigma™ permanent markers. They draw a very fine line and generally do not bleed. If you cannot find them in your local quilt shop, Pigma™ pens and labels are available through Wallflower Designs™.

Another choice is to use waste canvas if you do cross stitch. This canvas is used to keep the letters straight. Baste the waste canvas on top of your fabric. Cross stitch your name. Then wet the canvas and remove it. The only thing left is your nice, straight signature.

The signature area should include the following information: your first name, maiden name and married name; the year the project was made; the city, town, county and state where the project was made. The label may also include for whom or for what special occasion the project was made.

Here is an example: If the project is being made for a grandchild, the block on the top of the quilt could show for whom the quilt was made and by whom. It could include a special message like a poem or note. On the back of the quilt, a label should be placed showing the full name of the maker, date and location.

Signing the quilt adds to the value of the project in terms of sentiment and historical preservation.

## APPLIQUE WITH GLUE

You will now be ready to applique your pieced hexagons, the flower shape, to a 12½" x 12½" fabric background. With your glue stick, on the back of your hexagon design, rub the outer edge seam allowance area lightly. You only need a little glue to hold the seam allowance under. After a section is marked, roll the seam under so the edge is straight. The glue will hold the seam in place. Do a small section at a time to keep the glue moist while you work. If you try to glue the entire outer area, the glue could be dry before you are ready to turn under the seams. Work in a circular direction. After all edges are turned under, the hexagon design must be centered onto a background square.

Select a background that will contrast with the outer portion of the hexagon design. To center the design on the background square, draw diagonal lines on top of your background square with a removable marker.

Where the lines intersect is the center of the square. If you prefer not to mark the background fabric, you can finger crease the lines. When using this method, fold the background fabric in half and finger crease the center area. This is done by pinching the fabric between the thumbnail and first finger. Rub the thumbnail on the folded edge of the fabric. When you open the square, you should be able to see the crease in the center. Fold the fabric in the opposite direction and do the same; you will have a little plus sign in the center of the square. Find the center of the hexagon design also. Place a pin in the center of the hexagon design and then through the center of the background square, wrong side of the hexagon design against right side of background fabric. Secure the hexagon design to the background square. Two of the petals or leaves should be parallel with the sides of the background square. With your glue stick, lightly dab the back of the hexagon design and secure it to the background fabric. Remove the pin. Do the applique stitch around the outside edge of the hexagon design. Refer to the section below on helpful applique hints. Press the block after the applique is complete. Remember to lift the iron; *do not* slide it across the top of your applique work.

## HELPFUL HINTS FOR APPLIQUE

• The applique stitch should be kept small and even. If done properly, there will be little or no sign of the stitch on the surface (Fig. 2-4). Put a single knot on the end of the thread. I recommend using a thin English Sharp needle. The needle has a little give and allows you to keep your stitches small. Come up from the back of the project so the knots are under the background.

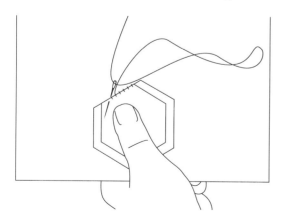

*Figure 2-4.*

When you come up, catch all of the work, the background and the outside edge of the applique piece. Always stay to the outside edge of the applique piece. Only pick up the outside thread on the applique fabric. The stitch is worked on the surface for the rest of the stitch. Take the needle back down right beside the previous stitch where you came up, only taking the background part of the stitch. Along with this, come back up and catch the outside edge of the applique work. Tug the stitch lightly so the applique piece is tight with the background; this helps to hide the stitch.

This stitch is taken on the diagonal. Tug gently at the end of each stitch. This seems to tuck it just slightly. To end the stitch, go back under the background and knot the thread. Figure 2-5 shows how the stitch will look on the back.

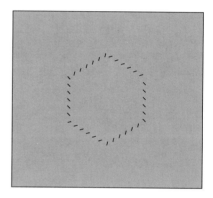

*Figure 2-5.*

• Use thread that matches your applique work, not the background fabric. Use a single strand of thread.

Applique patterns are usually numbered or lettered in the order they are to be placed on the background. This is to allow proper layering and appearance of the pattern.

• Press all of your applique work after completion by lifting the iron and putting it back down on each area. Do not slide the iron across the top of your applique work. The other alternative is to place a towel on your ironing board, place the block face down on the towel, and press the back of the block. I prefer this to pressing on the top.

• Cotton fabric is the easiest fabric to use for applique. Polyester fibers tend to straighten themselves and pull the applique stitch out. Applique is far too much work to risk your stitches working themselves out.

• There are two schools of thought on cutting the fabric behind the applique. Some people cut the background away from behind the applique work and others do not. There are differing philosophies on this matter. Some people feel the back should be cut away to make the piece flatter and easier to quilt. Others feel that cutting the back away weakens the block and could cause it to not be truly square (Fig. 2-6).

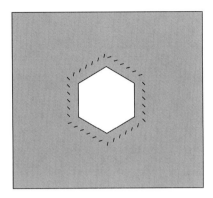

*Figure 2-6.*

• Cut the ends of your thread at an angle instead of straight. This makes it easier to thread the needle.

• If you are having a problem threading the needle, flip the needle around and try to thread from the opposite side of the eye. It will make a difference.

• Only cut the thread about 18" long so it does not knot when you are sewing.

• The way you hold your applique may make a difference. Some prefer to hold the piece so the applique is facing in toward their bodies, while others prefer to work with the applique piece away from their bodies. There really is a difference between these methods. Most do a better job using one method or the other.

## QUILTING IDEAS

If you are doing quilt-as-you-go, add the lattice to this block. In Figure 2-7 are ideas for quilting this block. If you are looking for simple ideas for quilting, refer to children's coloring books. They have some great and easy outlines.

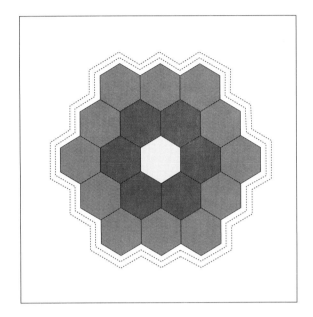

*Figure 2-7.*

# Lesson THREE

*Rail Fence:
Quick Piecing Straight Lines*

## TRADITIONAL PIECING

As with the Grandmother's Flower Garden, the Rail Fence pattern gives you a choice of two sizes. Let's start with the larger size (Fig. 3-1).

Make the template below (Fig. 3-2). Notice this template has two solid lines. When you see a pattern like this, you know that it already includes the seam allowance. The inside line is the sewing line and the outside line is the cutting line. The patterns in this book are shown in different ways. Books, patterns and magazines differ in their presentation of patterns. This layout should help you to become familiar with the possibilities.

Cut four of each of these patterns from four different fabrics. Arrange the fabrics from lightest to darkest with the darker fabrics to the inside. Switch and try the lighter fabric to the inside. Decide which arrangement you like. The block is broken down into four squares. Sew in units and rows (Fig. 3-3).

*Figure 3-1. Rail Fence Block.*

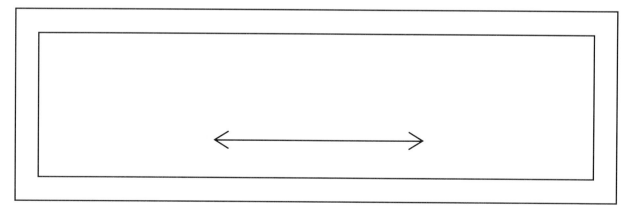

*Figure 3-2.*

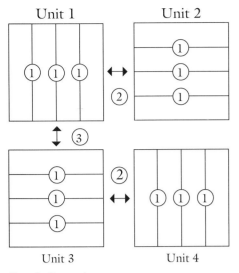

Unit 1      Unit 2

Unit 3      Unit 4

Step 1: Sew units.
Step 2: Sew units together.
Step 3: Sew rows together.

*Figure 3-3.*

Press the seams in the units toward the darker fabric. Press the seam for the top row in the opposite direction from the seam for the bottom row. This will allow the seams to butt. Press the center seam either up or down.

The second choice for the Rail Fence requires a smaller template (Fig. 3-4).

With the template below (Fig. 3-5), cut nine of each fabric. Arrange the fabric from lightest to darkest again.

*Figure 3-4. Rail Fence Block.*

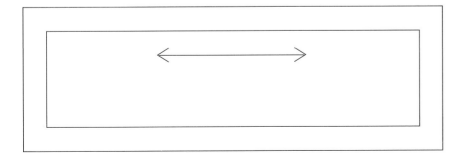

*Figure 3-5.*

There are nine units and three rows in the block (Fig. 3-6). Press all the unit seams toward the darker fabric. Press the seams in rows one and three in the same direction, then press row two in the opposite direction. Then sew the rows together and press those seams in one direction.

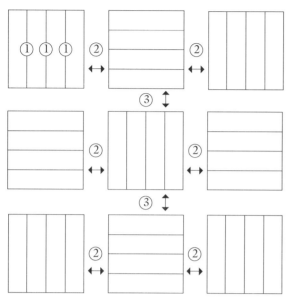

Step 1: Sew units

Step 2: Sew units together

Step 3: Sew rows together

*Figure 3-6.*

## QUICK PIECING
## FOR THE SMALLER SIZE UNIT

For the smaller size unit, cut one 1½" x 45" strip of all four fabrics. This measurement includes the seam allowances. If you are sewing by hand, mark your ¼" sewing lines on the inside of these lines. It is easier to mark before the fabric is cut. Sew the four strips together along their lengths, from the lighter to the darker fabric. Press the seams toward the darker fabric. Cut the pieced strip apart into 4½" squares, as shown in Fig. 3-7. You will need nine of these units. Arrange the blocks into the design and sew the rows together. This method, called strip piecing, saves a lot of time and is fun.

To strip piece or quick piece blocks for the large unit, cut strips 2" wide and cut 6½" squares.

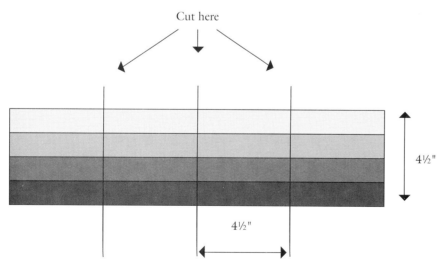

Cut here

4½"

4½"

*Figure 3-7.*

## QUILTING IDEAS FOR THE LARGER SIZE UNIT

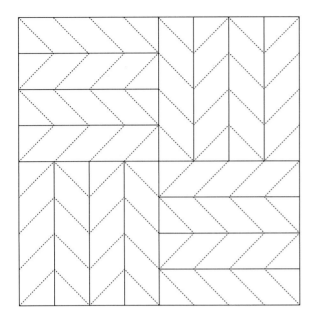

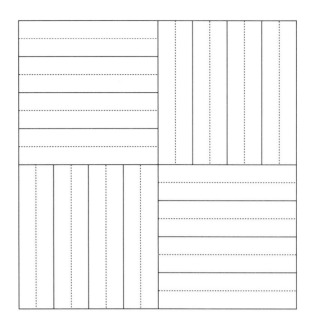

## QUILTING IDEAS FOR THE SMALLER SIZE UNIT

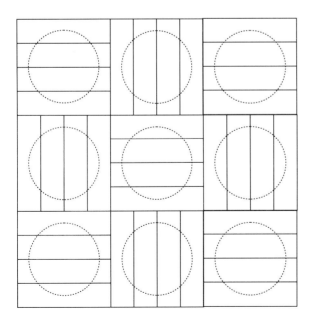

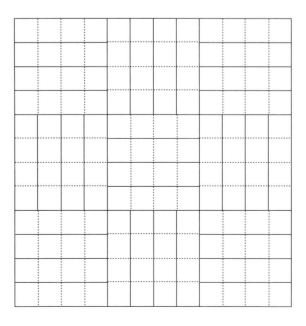

# Lesson FOUR

*Honey Bee:*
*Straight Piecing,*
*Freezer-Paper Applique,*
*and Window Templates*

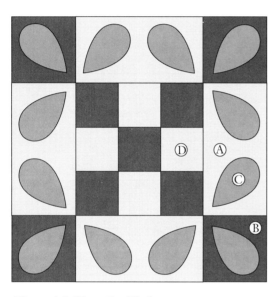

*Figure 4-1. Honey Bee Block.*

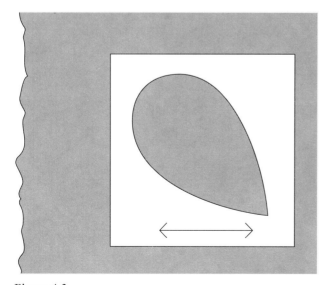

*Figure 4-2.*

To make this block, use the patterns in Fig. 4-3 to make templates and then:

Cut 4 of piece A

Cut 4 of piece B

Cut 12 of piece C

Cut 9 of piece D

Be sure the colors you choose for C contrast with the fabric behind it.

Cut five of piece D from one fabric and four from another fabric.

The window template is a two-fold template. The outside edges are used for sewing lines and the inside opening is used for placement of the applique pieces. Trace the lines for B and C on the same template. Cut template C away from the B template. This will leave an opening in the area where C should be (Fig. 4-2).

Sew the block in units and rows, as shown in Fig. 4-4.

After the block is pieced and pressed flat, you are ready to do the applique work. Using the window template, place the template on the surface of the block and move it from corner to corner, tracing the opening as you go. Be sure to use a marker that will wash out of the fabric, as it is being used on the surface.

There are two freezer-paper techniques I would like you to try on this block. The first is as follows:

## FREEZER-PAPER APPLIQUE: METHOD ONE

1. Place the freezer paper over pattern piece C and trace the finished size. Do not add seam allowance. Cut

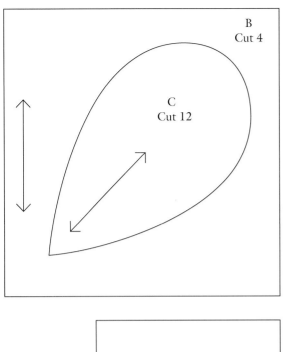

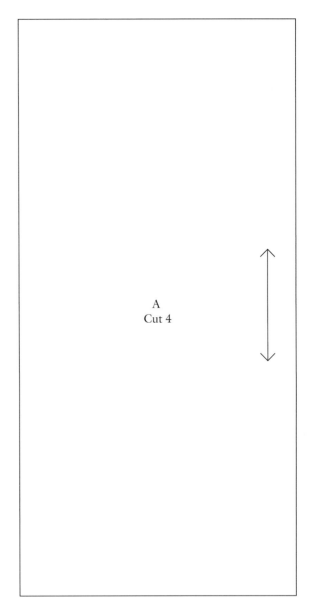

B
Cut 4

C
Cut 12

A
Cut 4

D
Cut 9

*Figure 4-3.*

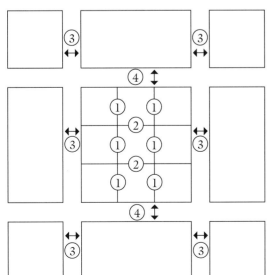

Step 1: Sew center rows.

Step 2: Sew large center unit.

Step 3: Sew rows together.

Step 4: Sew block together.

*Figure 4-4.*

49

piece C from freezer paper with your paper scissors.

2. Iron the freezer paper with the coated side down onto the back of the fabric. This freezer paper template can be used several times before it loses its stickiness.

3. As shown in Fig. 4-5, cut the fabric adding the ¼" seam allowance.

4. Use a dry iron and roll the seam allowance up over the freezer paper, creating a crease of the design around the edges (b). Remove the freezer paper from the back before step 5.

a         b

*Figure 4-5.*

5. Turn the edges under with your needle or use a glue stick. If you are using the glue stick, remember to lightly dab the back of the fabric on the seam allowance area only. It only takes a small amount of glue to hold the fabric down. You have to manipulate the seams so there are no points on the curves. Use your fingers to roll the seam allowance toward the back. The fullness should be in toward the inside of the piece. Press the piece flat.

6. Secure piece C either by pinning or gluing in place. You do not want piece C to shift during the applique process.

7. Applique stitch the edge of piece C to the piece behind it.

## FREEZER-PAPER APPLIQUE: METHOD TWO

1. Cut a freezer-paper template with no seam allowance.

2. Cut the fabric applique piece with a ¼" seam allowance.

3. Center the freezer-paper template over the applique piece with the coated side facing up toward you (Fig. 4-6a).

4. With the use of a dry iron, heat the seam allowance onto the freezer paper. It will adhere to the freezer paper. (In Fig. 4-6, b is the top view and c is the back view.)

5. Applique the design to the background, leaving the paper in place. After stitching about seven-eights of the way around, pull the freezer paper away and close the opening. Be sure to leave the opening on the side, and not on the curve or bottom point.

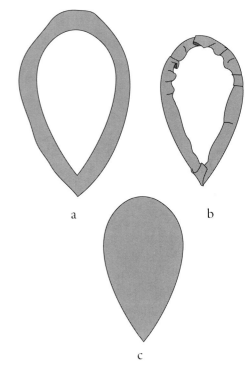

a         b

c

*Figure 4-6.*

## HELPFUL APPLIQUE HINTS

• If you are using pins to secure the piece to the background, place the pins into the wrong side of the background fabric. Putting the pins in the back will prevent the thread from getting wrapped around the pins while you are doing the applique stitch.

• If you are doing method one and not using pins, try using glue to hold the piece in place. You only need a small amount of glue.

• Whichever method you use to secure the piece in place, be sure your applique piece is flat on the background. You do not want any shifting of the applique piece during stitching.

• When turning points, there are some things that will make it easier. Turn the point first, by flipping it straight in toward the applique piece and then roll the seam allowance over on the sides (Fig. 4-7).

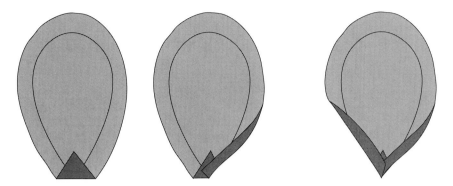

*Figure 4-7.*

• If you ever have a problem with the freezer paper not coming off the fabric, put the applique piece in the freezer for a while and it will release itself.

## QUILTING IDEAS

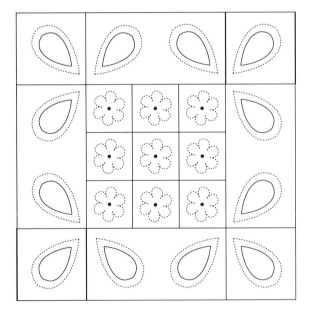

# Lesson FIVE

## Oak Leaf Reel: Buttonhole Stitch Method of Applique

*Figure 5-1. Oak Leaf Reel Block.*

This pattern looks harder than it really is. With this block, we will learn another applique technique. Instead of turning the edges under like the traditional methods of applique, we will do a buttonhole stitch on the raw edges.

Cut a 12½" x 12½" background square. Be sure your background contrasts with the fabric to be used for the Oak Leaf. Cut a 9" x 9" piece of fabric to be used for the Oak Leaf.

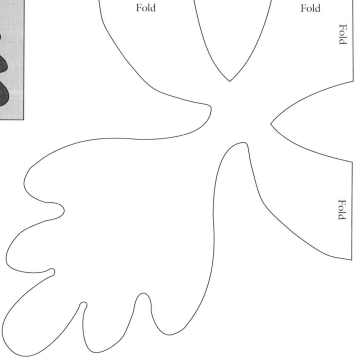

Fold    Fold    Fold    Fold

*Figure 5-2.*

Make a template from freezer paper or regular paper using the pattern in Fig. 5-2. Do not add a seam allowance to the template. The pattern may look funny to you now, but just wait until you see the outcome.

Fold the 9" square in half, and then in half again. Now the fabric is four layers thick (Fig. 5-3).

*Figure 5-4.*

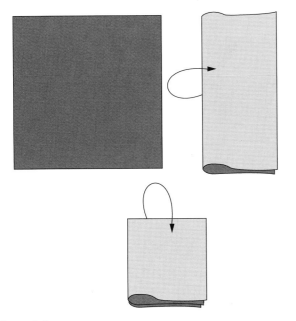

*Figure 5-3.*

If you are using freezer paper, iron it onto the top of the fabric, making sure the fold areas of the template are on the folds of the fabric (Fig. 5-4). You may want to mark the word "fold" on the template to ensure you place it correctly on the fabric. If using regular paper, pin the template to the top of the fabric, being sure it is very secure through all four layers.

Cut along the edge of the template. Do not cut along the fold. Do not add a seam allowance to the fabric. Open the pattern and you will see the entire Oak Leaf pattern. See, that was easy.

To find the center of your background fabric, use your ruler and removable marking pencil, mark the diagonal lines from corner to corner in both directions. Where the lines intersect is the center (Fig. 5-5).

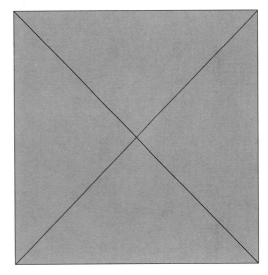

*Figure 5-5.*

The Oak Leaf design is placed on these diagonal lines. Find the center of the Oak Leaf and secure it on top of the background.

Use your glue stick to secure the Oak Leaf to the background (Fig. 5-6). You want the Oak Leaf to be very secure. You will have problems if it shifts while you are doing the buttonhole stitch.

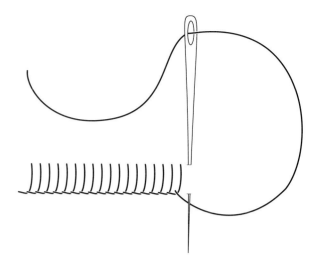

*Figure 5-7.*

Applique done with this stitch holds up very well with washing. I have a wallhanging made with this technique that hangs over a heat duct in my kitchen. It needs cleaning often but shows no signs of fraying.

Any of the applique patterns in the back of the book can be done with the buttonhole stitch.

## QUILTING IDEAS

On page 55 are several possible quilting designs for this block. When the applique design is repeated around its outside edges in quilting, it is called Echo Quilting.

The quilting lines can be transferred by placing the quilting design under the finished piece and tracing the lines. If the fabric is too dark or too busy, try holding it up to a window. If this method works, trace the design from the book onto a plain white piece of paper with a black felt tip pen. Tape the paper to the window and then tape the block over the paper. Trace the lines onto the background fabric with a marker that will wash from the fabric.

A way of transferring the design onto dark background fabric, would be to make a template from freezer paper, iron it onto the background fabric and trace the outline.

*Figure 5-6.*

Now for the buttonhole stitch, which is sometimes called the blanket stitch. Use a color of thread that blends with your Oak Leaf fabric and not the background, especially if this is your first time doing the stitch. Start with the center edges and work toward the outside edges. This stitch is generally worked from left to right. While holding the thread with your thumb, make a straight downward stitch. The needle should go over the thread and pull the stitch (Fig. 5-7). Be careful not to pull the stitch too tight or the piece will not lie flat. If you are having a problem with pulling the stitches too tight, try an embroidery hoop to help with the tension. The bottom line of the stitch will lie on the raw edge of the fabric and the vertical stitch should be on the inside of the Oak Leaf. Keep the vertical lines straight and even. The stitches should be approximately ⅛" in on the Oak Leaf and approximately ⅛" or less apart.

# Lesson Six

## Applique of Hearts: Applique with Interfacing and Diagonal Sets

*Figure 6-1.*

This pattern is easy. Don't let the fact that it is on the diagonal fool you. It is all straight line sewing. Tilt the block a quarter of a turn and it is easier to see how to sew the units and rows. The diagram on page 58 shows you how to piece the block easily.

Using the patterns on page 57, make templates for shapes A-D, and cut the fabric pieces indicated.

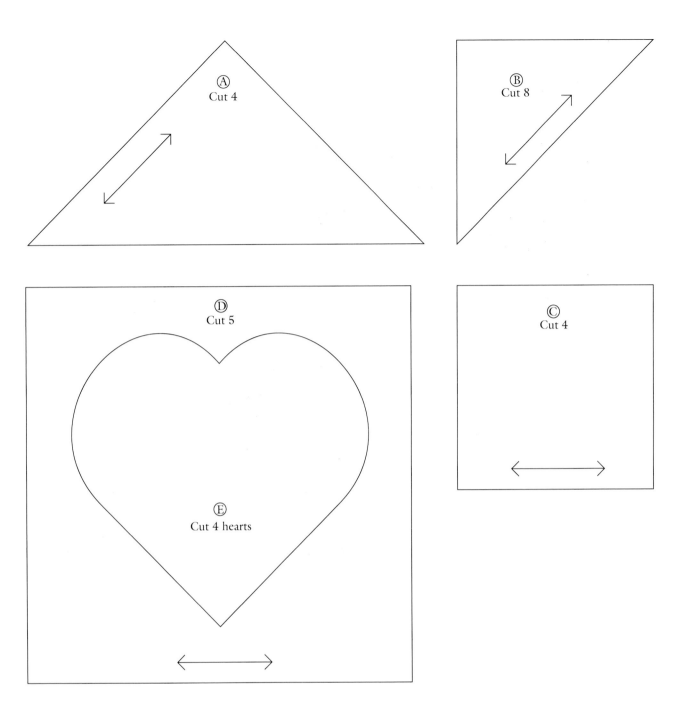

*Figure 6-2.*

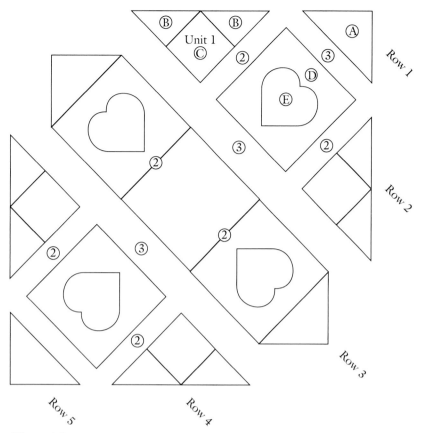

*Figure 6-3.*

There are four unit 1's. You are sewing a B piece to each side of a C piece. Press the seams away from C. After the units are built, start sewing the rows. There are five rows (Fig. 6-3).

1. Sew the four unit 1's
2. Sew rows together
3. Sew block together

After the block is pieced, applique the hearts on top of the D pieces. Interfacing is the applique technique to be used on this block.

1. Cut the fabric and the interfacing with a ¼" seam allowance. *Do not use iron-on interfacing.*

2. Place the heart of interfacing and the heart of fabric front-to-front. With the sewing machine, sew on the sewing line the entire way around.

3. Clip into the cleavage of the heart to about two threads from the cleavage. Cut straight into the cleavage. Clip all the way around the heart shape, into the seam allowance area.

4. Next, cut an opening in the middle of the back of the interfacing and turn the piece inside out.

5. Use some kind of turner to round the edges. There is a plastic turner used by dressmakers that can be used.

6. Press the heart flat.

7. Then piece the block following instructions at left.

8. Secure the heart to piece D and applique stitch around the edge.

## HELPFUL APPLIQUE HINTS

When clipping the cleavage on deep valleys, clip straight into the cleavage and about two threads away from the seam line. Do not clip to the seam because this may cause weakness on the raw edges. Also, remember to take some close stitches at these areas to secure them and to prevent raw edges from fraying.

# Lesson SEVEN

*Eight Pointed Star:
Straight Piecing
and Set-Ins*

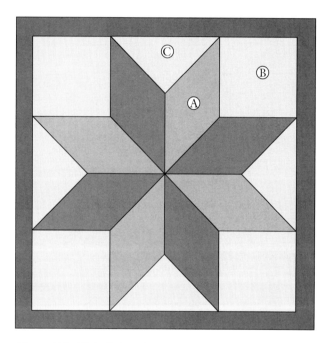

*Figure 7-1. Eight Pointed Star Block (3" diamond).*

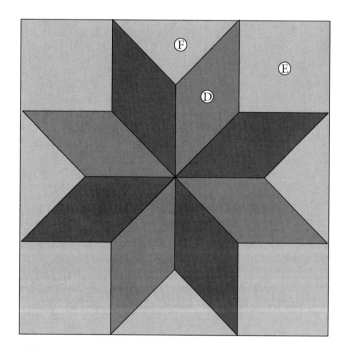

*Figure 7-2. Eight Pointed Star (3½" diamond).*

This is one of the few blocks that is pieced differently by hand and machine sewers. Each set of directions is designed to make it easier for one method of piecing. Whichever method you select (machine or hand piecing), you have a choice of working with a 3" diamond or a 3½" diamond. The 3" diamond allows for an inner border (Fig. 7-1). The border will be 1" finished. Therefore, the border will be cut 1½" wide to allow for the seam. Cut two strips 10½" long and two

strips 12½" long. The 3½" diamond will make a 12" block which does not need a border before the lattice (Fig. 7-2).

Select the size diamond you want to use and cut eight. Cut four triangles for the sides of the star and four squares for the corners of the star. If you are using the 3" diamond, cut the square and the triangle for the 3" star. If you are using the 3½" diamond, use the square and triangle for the 3½" star.

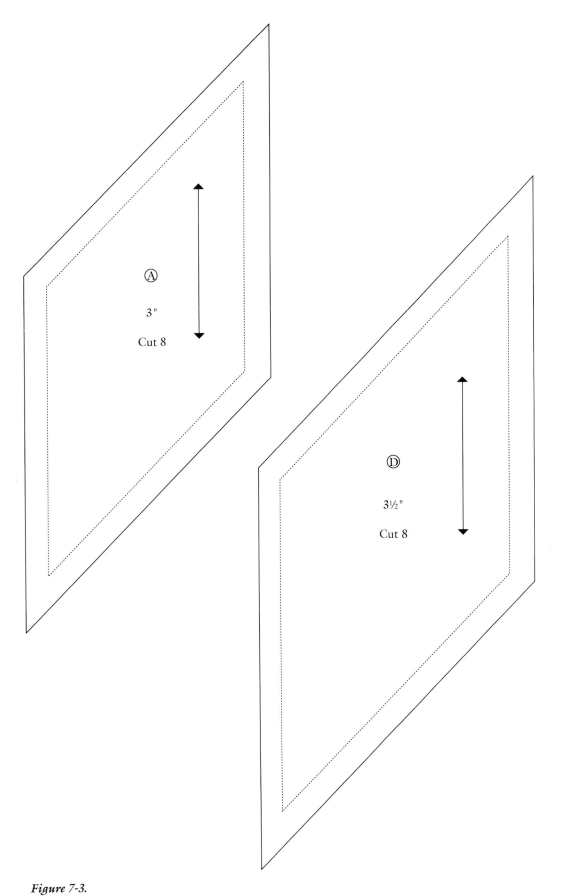

Ⓐ

3"

Cut 8

Ⓓ

3½"

Cut 8

*Figure 7-3.*

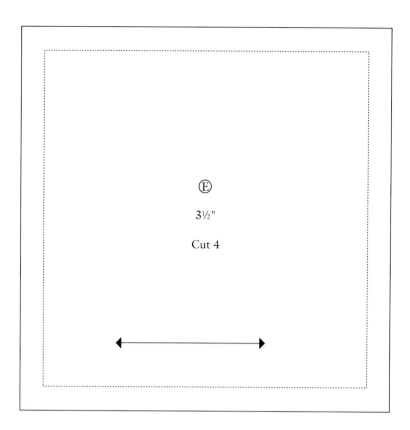

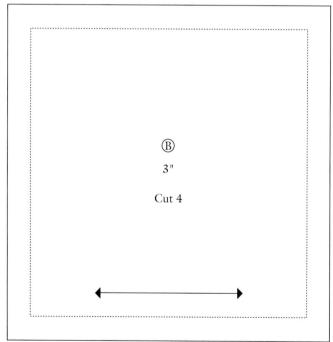

*Figure 7-4.*

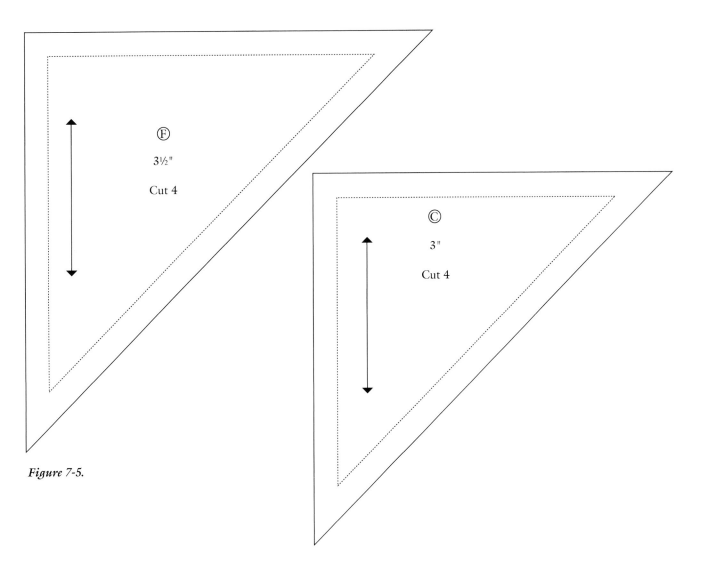

(F)

3½"

Cut 4

(C)

3"

Cut 4

*Figure 7-5.*

## HAND SEWING THE BLOCK

Sew the diamonds in units of two. There are three ways to make the points come together in the middle.

When sewing all of these seams on the diamonds, sew from the outside to the inside, where all of the points come together. When you are about ½" from the center, cross over the sewing line, increasing the seam allowance and decreasing the size of the diamond. Only cross over by the width of the needle. This will remove some of the fullness from the center and make the block lie flatter (Fig. 7-6).

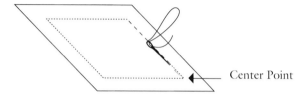

Center Point

*Figure 7-6.*

After the units are sewn, press the seams. The seams should all be pressed in a circular fashion (Fig. 7-7). The tails should be clipped from the center points. Removing this excess material makes it easier to get the points to meet.

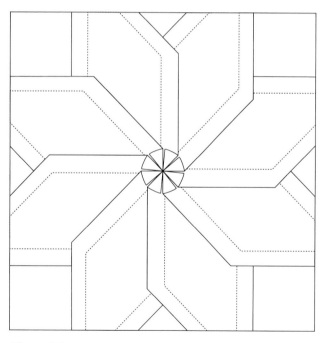

*Figure 7-7.*

The squares and triangles are added as set-ins. These are usually easier for hand sewers, so if this is your first time for set-ins, I highly recommend doing them by hand. Setting-in is required when you need to sew a piece into an angle.

Pin the three points. This will feel awkward because of the fullness, but it will work out fine. Sew into the point, lift the seam, do a backstitch and sew out to the other point. If you find this method too difficult, sew one seam into the point and knot at the center point. Then pin and sew the other seam. Press the seams in toward the diamonds.

This picture shows where the three points would be pinned and the arrows show the direction of sewing (Fig. 7-8).

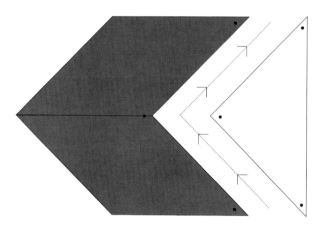

*Figure 7-8.*

## MACHINE SEWING THE BLOCK

Machine sewing the star is not difficult either, if you follow these directions. Set-ins are more difficult on the machine so do as few of them as possible. Start by sewing the triangles to the diamonds (Fig. 7-9). The seams are sewn from the outside to the inside. Sew a triangle to a diamond. Only sew to the ¼" seam and backstitch. Press the seam away from the diamond. Attach the second diamond to the triangle and the first diamond being sure to stop sewing at the previous sewing lines. Press the seam away from the diamond. Make four of these units.

*Figure 7-9.*

Add a square to the corner of two of these units (Fig. 7-10).

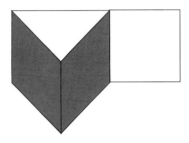

*Figure 7-10.*

Sew a diamond unit to Figure 7-10. Make two of these (Fig. 7-11).

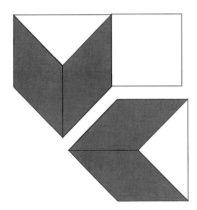

*Figure 7-11.*

Sew a square to the two ends of one of the units from the step above (Fig. 7-12).

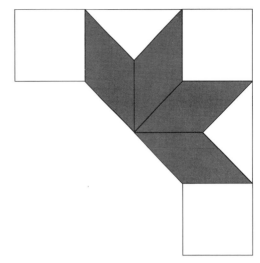

*Figure 7-12.*

Sew these two units together. Sew the diamonds first. Then close the seams along the square (Fig. 7-13).

*Figure 7-13.*

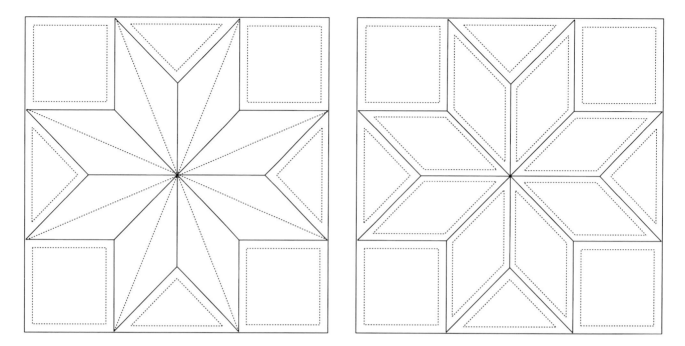

# Lesson EIGHT

## Drunkard's Path and Variations: Curved Seams

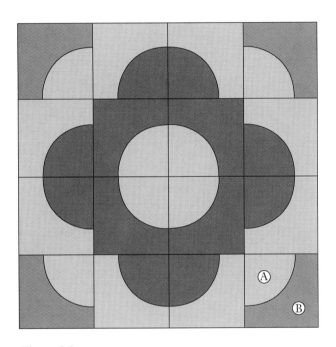

Figure 8-1.

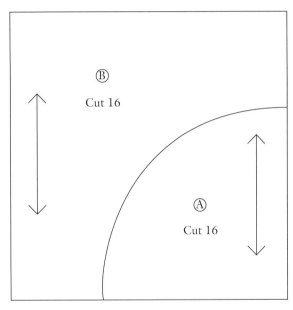

Figure 8-2.

There are many different layouts for this design. On page 69 are some of the many possible variations. You may select any of the designs because, in each, you must piece a curve. Rose Marie Allison, a friend and fellow quilter, liked the idea so much that she did a Sampler quilt of nothing but different Drunkard's Path variations. Each block looks so very different that, at first sight, you might not notice they are all variations of the same pattern.

As you look at this design (Fig. 8-1), you will notice that there are four rows with four units in each row.

Each unit has a concave curve (piece B) and a convex curve (piece A).

Make a template for A and B (Fig. 8-2). Add the ¼" seam allowance to the fabric, not the template. The seam allowance on the curve must be accurate. This will make the piecing of the curve much easier. One way to make the seam accurate is to use the ½" wheel. There is an illustration of the wheel being used on page 19. Roll the wheel along the edge of the plastic template on the curve area. I use my ruler on the straight lines. Cut as many of each color as you need for the design of your choice.

Find the center of both of the curved fabric pieces by folding them in half at the curve and finger creasing the exact center (Fig. 8-3). Place the pieces front-to-front. This will feel more awkward than anything we have done so far. It looks as if the pieces will never go together, but they will, and quite easily.

You can start pinning the pieces together in three places. Put a pin in the center of the two pieces and secure the pin. One of the tricks to securing the pin is

to only take a small amount of fabric in the pin, about two threads. Now, pin the two ends. If you are hand piecing, it is easier to work with only these three pins. However, if you are machine piecing, place several pins on the curve. On the first unit, sew with the concave side facing towards you; and on the second unit, sew with the convex side facing towards you. Most people find working from one side much easier than from the other.

The heavier fabric generally pushes the curved seam to one side or the other. Unless you have to press toward the darker fabric, just let the seam go to the side of its choice and press it flat.

Sew the block into units and then rows. Press the seams for rows one and three in one direction and rows two and four in the opposite direction. Sew the rows to make the block, pressing those seams either up or down.

*Figure 8-3.*

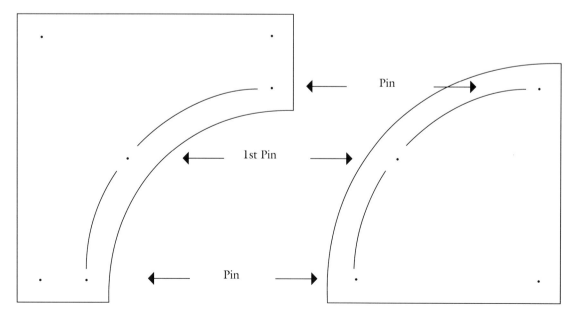

*Figure 8-4.*

# QUILTING IDEAS

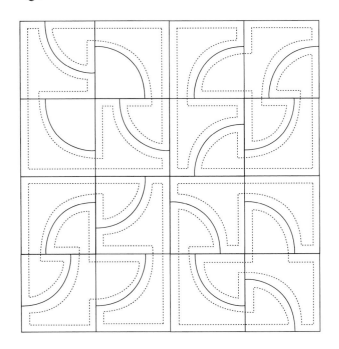
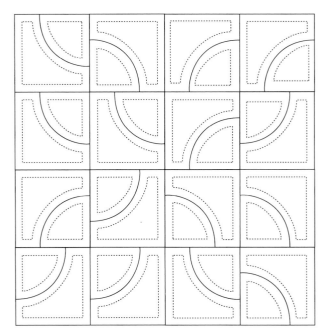

# DRUNKARD'S PATH VARIATIONS

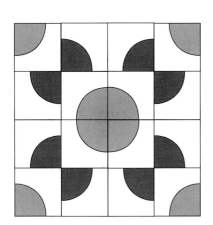

# Lesson NINE

## Bridal Wreath: Poster-Board Techniques, Bias-Bar Stems and Circles

*Figure 9-1. Bridal Wreath Block.*

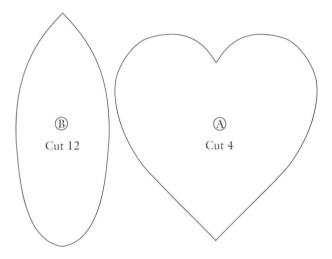

*Figure 9-2.*

With this design (Fig. 9-1), you will learn another applique technique and also learn how to make bias strips for circles or stems. The supplies you will need for this design are poster board, liquid spray starch, Q-Tips or small stencil brush, an iron, and bias bars.

Cut a piece of background fabric 12½" x 12½"; this measurement includes seam allowances. Be sure the fabric will contrast nicely with the pieces to be appliqued on top. Make templates for piece A, the heart, then cut piece B, the leaf (Fig. 9-2).

Cut four hearts and twelve leaves from the fabric.

Find the center of the background fabric. Draw a horizontal line and a vertical line through the center, instead of the diagonal lines drawn in the previous design. Using the heart template, trace the placement of the heart pieces. The center point of the hearts will be in the exact center of the background square (Fig. 9-3).

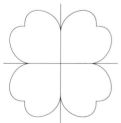

*Figure 9-3.*

We are going to use the poster-board technique for these applique pieces. This technique was taught to me by Pat Andreatta. In her book, *Applique Can Be Easy*, Pat explains this technique in detail. She also has several other books with wonderful applique designs. If you like applique, her books are a must.

1. Cut a template from poster board. Do not add a seam allowance to the template.

2. Cut a fabric heart, adding the ¼" seam allowance.

3. Take out your liquid spray starch, Q-Tips and iron. First, put a towel on top of your ironing-board cover and then place a piece of scrap fabric on top of the towel so the cover will not get stained. Spray a little starch into a small dish. Working on your protected ironing board, place the poster board template in the center on the wrong side of the fabric heart.

4. Clip straight into the cleavage of the heart. Stop two threads away from the cleavage.

5. Start this technique at the cleavage. Dip the Q-Tip into the spray starch and then with the Q-Tip, wet a small section of the seam allowance. If you have a small stencil brush, it can be used in place of a Q-Tip.

6. With the dry iron, roll the seam allowance up over the edge of the poster board template. Let the iron sit. You must allow the spray starch to dry for this technique to work. Do not push down on the iron, simply let it sit on the fabric. It will not burn the fabric in the time it takes to dry the starch. This may take a little practice before you feel comfortable; it is our nature not to allow the iron to sit. The spray starch hardens and holds the seam allowance in place (Fig. 9-4).

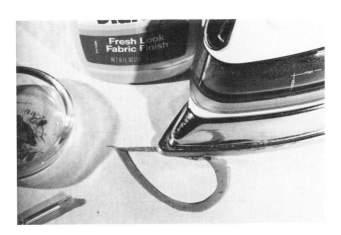

*Figure 9-4.*

7. Turn the bottom point straight up and in. Fold one side of the seam allowance over and then the other. This way there are no raw edges at the bottom.

8. Remove the poster board and you are ready to applique the heart in place.

The next step for the Bridal Wreath is the bias circle. This piece needs to be cut on the bias to allow the fabric to ease around the circle. This technique can be used for flower stems or basket handles.

Cut a strip of fabric on the bias. Try to cut the piece long enough so that you only have one seam where you start and stop, but none in the middle. The easiest way to do this is to place your fabric on a flat surface. Fold one corner up until the fold is as long as you need the bias strip. For this block you want a strip 24" long, as shown in Fig. 9-5.

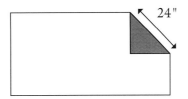

*Figure 9-5.*

Cut the strip 1¼" wide. This includes a ¼" seam allowance. Fold the strip lengthwise, back to back and sew the seam closed. Trim the seam allowance from ¼" to ⅛". (You do not have to turn this tube inside out.)

Insert a bias bar that is ⅜" wide through the tube. Fold the seam towards the back. Wet the seam with the Q-Tip and starch. Dry with the iron. Keep moving the bias bar down the tube on the inside. After you have pressed the entire seam, pull the bias bar from the tube.

Draw a circle for the placement of the bias circle. If you have a compass, use it. If you do not have a compass, find something circular like a plate or saucer. If your background fabric is light enough, lay it over the pattern and trace the lines onto the background fabric.

You are now ready to applique the circle in place. Applique the inner fold first, then applique the outside fold. Where the seams meet, tuck the raw edge inside the opening about ¼" and sew the seam closed. Press the circle flat.

Mark the placement for the leaves. If your background fabric is lighter, simply trace the design as shown below (Fig. 9-6). You may need to darken the lines on the pattern below with a black felt-tip pen, so they are dark enough to show through your background fabric.

If you are working with a darker background fabric, make a template of freezer paper and iron it on the background fabric. With a white pencil, trace the placement of the leaves (Fig. 9-7).

After the placement lines are marked, you are ready to applique the leaves in place. Remove the freezer paper and applique the leaves. This step takes time but you will feel great satisfaction when you are finished.

*Figure 9-7.*

*Figure 9-6. This is ¼ of the total design.*

# Lesson TEN

## Flower Basket:
## Perfect Circles and
## Needle-Turn Applique

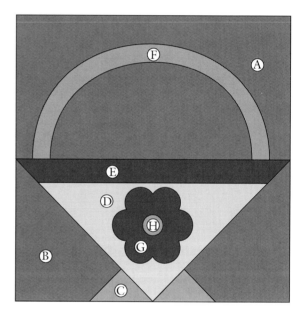

*Figure 10-1. Flower Basket Block.*

There are many popular basket patterns. Here is one that combines piecing and applique. You will learn a different way of working with bias strips on this basket handle, a technique I have found to work very well. The handle is smooth when completed (Fig. 10-1).

Piece A is 12" x 6" when finished.

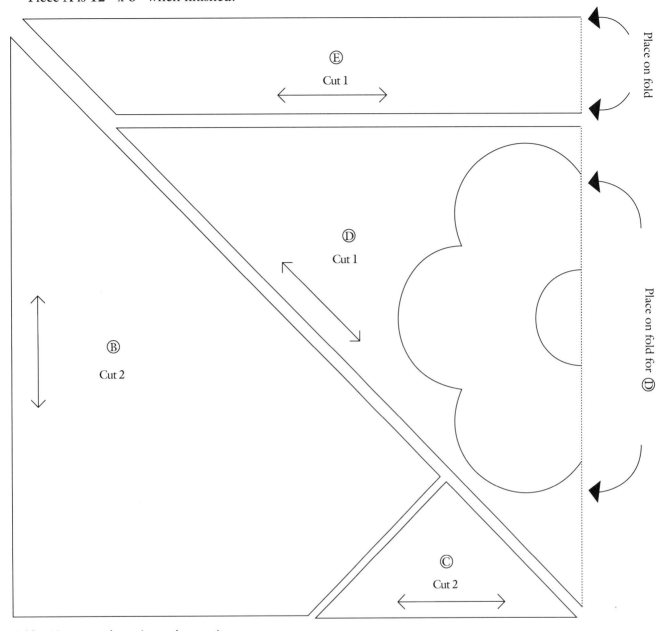

Place on fold

Place on fold for Ⓓ

Ⓔ
Cut 1

Ⓓ
Cut 1

Ⓑ
Cut 2

Ⓒ
Cut 2

Add a ¼" seam to these pieces when cutting.

*Figure 10-2.*

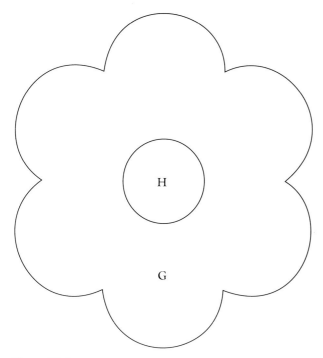

*Figure 10-3.*

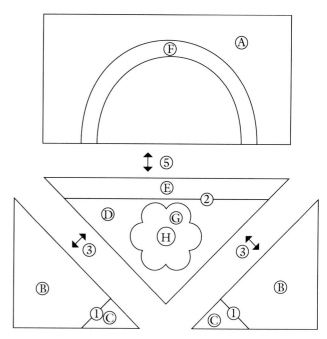

*Figure 10-4.*

Make a template for pieces A, B, C, D, E, G and H (Fig. 10-2, Fig. 10-3). For template A, make a 12½" x 6½" rectangle. Do not make a template for piece F. When cutting piece B, cut two templates, one as it is drawn and one in reverse. To cut in reverse, simply turn the template over (flip it upside down) and trace around the template to give you the reverse of the first piece.

1. As shown in Fig. 10-4, sew C to B. There are two of these units. Press those seams toward B.

2. Sew E to D. Press seam toward D.

3. Sew units from step one to the units from step two. Press seams toward the basket.

4. Make a template the size of the opening under the basket handle to be used as a placement for bias strip F, the basket handle (Fig. 10-5). Make the template using the placement guide on the next page (Fig. 10-6), tracing along the inside edge of the basket handle only.

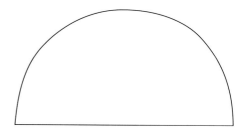

*Figure 10-5.*

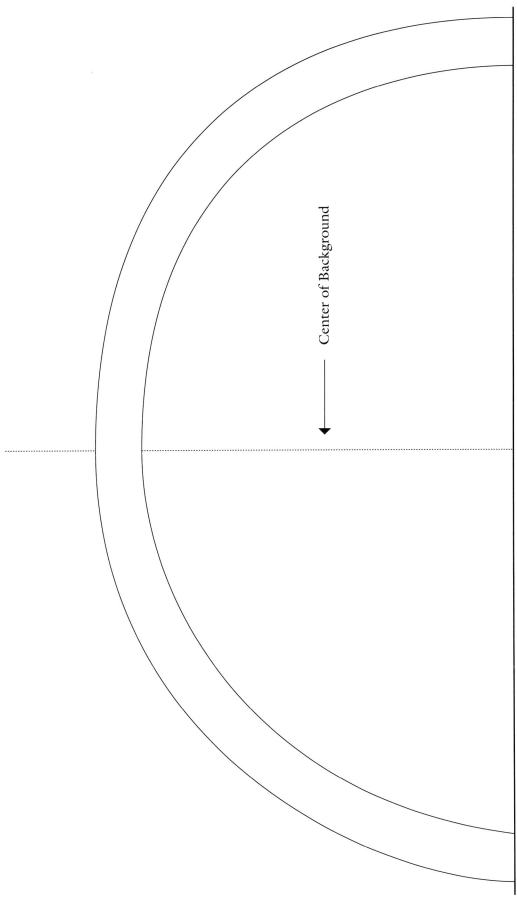

Center of Background

*Figure 10-6.*

Center the handle placement template on piece A and trace along the curve. Next, we are going to make a bias strip for the handle. Refer to the previous lesson on how to make bias strips. Cut the handle 16" long and 1½" wide.

We will try a different way of putting this handle down than we did the bias circle in the previous lesson.

Fold the bias strip in half lengthwise, wrong sides together, and press. The strip will be 16" long and ¾" wide.

The handle will be pinned in place with the raw edges facing up and the folded edge facing the basket. Sew along the raw edge with a ¼" seam allowance (Fig. 10-7). Be careful not to stretch the handle. Do not pull it as you sew. Be gentle.

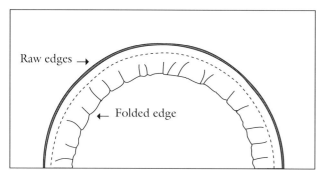

*Figure 10-7.*

With the iron on a light steam setting, push the folded edge up and over the raw edges. The steam will help push the bias handle flat onto piece A. Pin the handle flat and applique stitch on the folded side of the handle (Fig. 10-8).

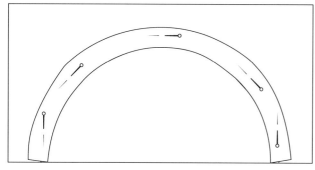

*Figure 10-8.*

5. Sew the unit for step 4 to the previous section. Press the seam toward the bottom of the basket.

6. Applique the flower in place. The flower must be appliqued before the circle. Try the needleturn technique with the flower.

A. Cut the fabric with a ¼" seam allowance. Clip into the cleavage areas until you are two threads away from the cleavage.

B. Center the flower on top of piece D; either pin or glue stick in place. If using glue, keep the glue toward the center. You do not want any glue along the raw edges.

C. With the tip of your needle, turn under small sections at a time.

D. Applique each small section as you turn it.

7. The last step for the Flower Basket is the circle.

A. Cut a circle from a piece of poster board. The circle must have smooth curves. You can use a fingernail file or emery board to smooth the edges.

B. Cut a circle from your fabric with a ¼" seam allowance.

C. Baste around the fabric-circle seam allowance about ⅛" from the edge. Keep the stitches pretty small.

D. Place the poster-board template on the back, in the center of the fabric circle. Pull the basting stitch. It will wrap the seam allowance around the template. Press the back of the circle (Fig. 10-9).

E. Remove the poster board and applique the circle in place.

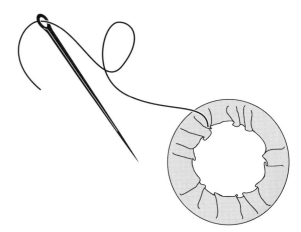

*Figure 10-9.*

# Lesson ELEVEN

## Star of Hearts: Finger Creased Applique

*Figure 11-1. Star of Hearts Block.*

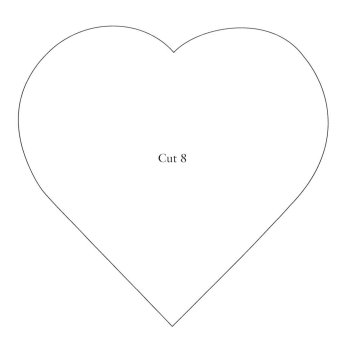

Cut 8

*Figure 11-2. Template for Heart.*

This block is really fun and easy (Fig. 11-1). The star in the center takes form after the applique is complete. Several of my students have used a large flower print in the center of each heart and a solid or small print in the center for the star. The effect is wonderful. Enjoy!

You will need the following:

1. A 12½" x 12½" piece of background fabric. Be sure it contrasts well with the fabric you choose for the hearts.

2. A 9" x 9" square for the center star design. This should also contrast well with the heart fabric.

3. Eight hearts (Fig. 11-2). Trace around each heart on the right side of the fabric with a removable marker and add a ¼" seam.

Find the center of the star fabric and secure it to the center of the background with your glue stick.

Mark the horizontal, vertical and diagonal lines on this block as shown in Fig. 11-3. These lines will be used for the placement of the hearts.

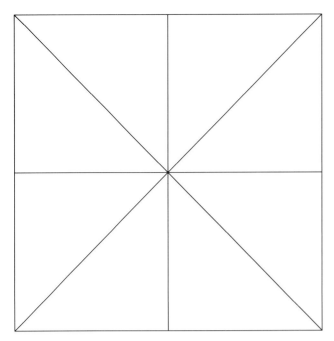

*Figure 11-3.*

For the applique of the hearts try the finger-creasing technique.

1. Clip the cleavage of the heart to within two threads of the cleavage.

2. While holding the heart, use your thumb to gently crease the seams under. Be careful not to pull the fabric out of shape, especially on the bias areas.

3. Secure the hearts to the background.

Place one heart on each of the centering lines. The hearts are positioned approximately 2" from the center (Fig. 11-4). Be sure to keep the cleavage on the line and the point at the bottom of the heart on the same line. Yours may be a little different, depending on how your seam allowance was turned. Adjust the hearts so they touch, but don't overlap. Pin them in place.

As you applique each heart into place, cut away from beneath the heart any excess fabric from the 9" square. Where the hearts meet, trim away the excess 9" square underneath, leaving a ¼" seam allowance to turn under.

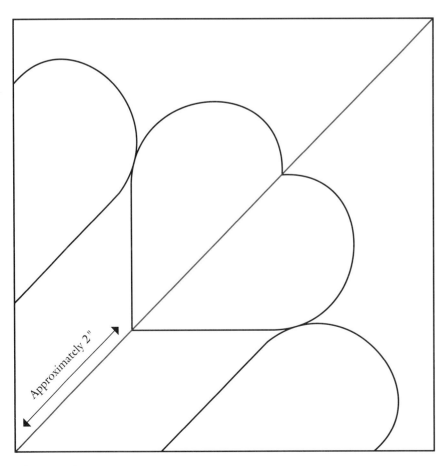

*Figure 11-4.*

# Lesson TWELVE

## *Tumbling Blocks or Baby's Blocks: Intermediate Set-Ins*

*Figure 12-1.*

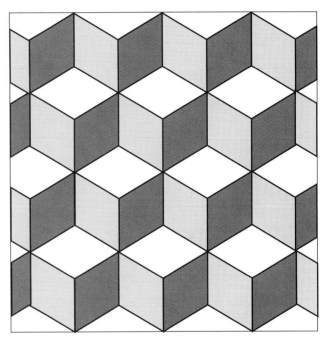

*Figure 12-2.*

You can use several different layouts with the Tumbling Blocks or Baby's Blocks design. You can sew seven blocks together and lay them out, as in figure 12-1.

You can sew enough blocks together to have a continuous design, as in figure 12-2.

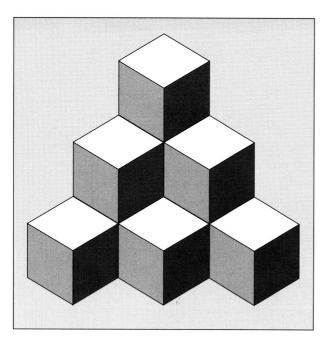

*Figure 12-3.*

You can also stack six blocks, as in figure 12-3.

Choosing the colors can be fun. The blocks should consist of three fabrics. Be sure the background contrasts with the block fabrics if you are doing one of the applique designs instead of the continuous design. The fabric you choose for a certain position on the block should be the same in every block. If you choose a brown fabric for the bottom left side of the block, the bottom left side of all the blocks should be done using that same brown fabric. By placing the fabrics in the same position, the design will take on a three-dimensional look.

This is the template to be used no matter which layout you pick (Fig. 12-4).

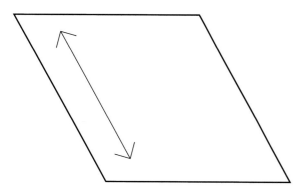

*Figure 12-4.*

For any design you choose, the blocks will be put together the same way. Sew the bases of the blocks together (Fig. 12-5).

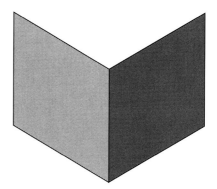

*Figure 12-5.*

The top diamond will be set in just like the set-ins you did for the Eight-Pointed Star. If you are sewing by hand, pin the points and sew from one point to the center point, then out to the last point (Fig. 12-6).

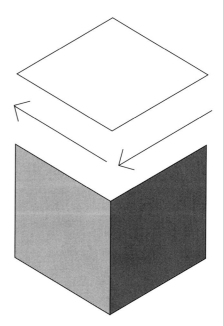

*Figure 12-6.*

If you are sewing by machine, you can either do it the same as the hand sewing method or you can sew from the outside to the inside point. Backstitch at the center point and remove the piece from the sewing machine. Then pin and sew from the outside to the inside of the other point.

Set the blocks in rows according to the design you choose (Fig. 12-7).

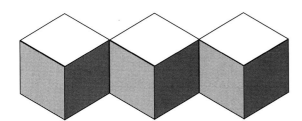

*Figure 12-7.*

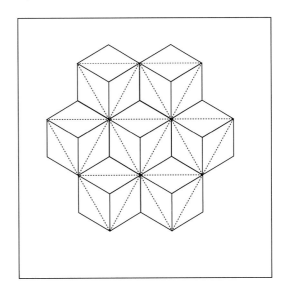

Now, sew the rows together. Pin row one to row two and so on. This may feel awkward because of the set-ins, but be patient and handle the blocks with care. I have always felt this step was easier to do by hand.

Center the design and applique the raw edges if you are doing one of the applique designs (Fig. 12-1, or Fig. 12-3). Mark the outside raw edges (on the right side of the fabric) with the ¼" seam so you can see where to turn the fabric under.

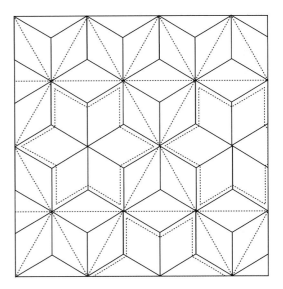

If you are making the continuous design, square off the outside edges and run a basting stitch around the outside edge of the 12" square. Cut away any excess fabric from the outside edge. Remember the block should be cut 12½" x 12½" (this includes the seam allowance).

Do you notice the Six-Pointed stars that are formed? Have fun working with this idea in mind!

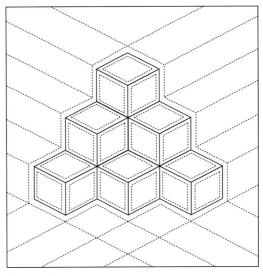

*Figure 12-8.*

# Lesson THIRTEEN

## Castle Wall:
## Eight Pointed Star
## and Set-Ins

*Figure 13-1. Castle Wall Block*

One of the things that makes this block fun is the choice of fabrics. In Fig. 13-1, you see the same pattern repeated in pieces E and B. I like the effect this gives to the pattern. Another idea that has been successful is to place a flower from the fabric in the D pieces, using the same flower repeatedly. The first Castle Wall block I made included striped fabric. By cutting the strip from the exact same place on the fabric, you can create a hexagon design in the center of this pattern. Whatever your choice, have fun with your fabric.

There are five different templates to be made for this design:

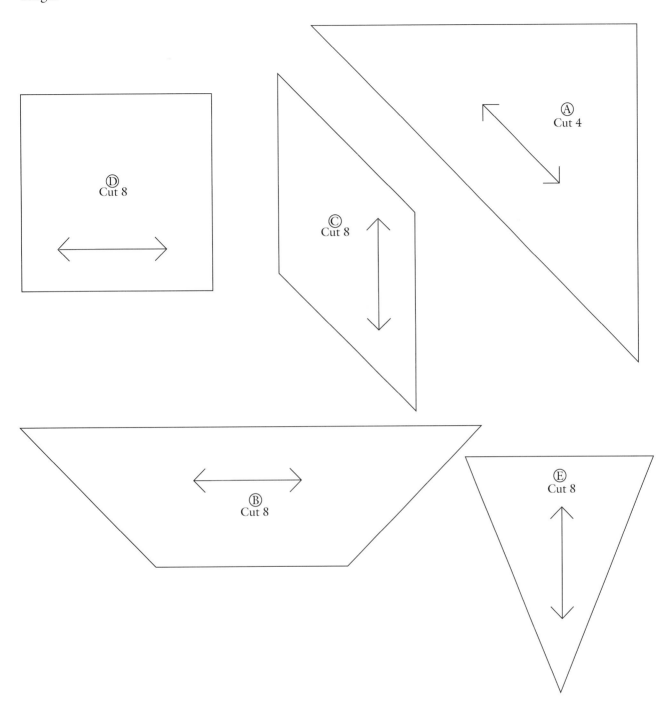

*Figure 13-2.*

There are three different units to make for this pattern (Fig. 13-3). Unit one consists of a C piece sewn to each side of a D piece. Press those seams toward the D pieces. Attach an A piece to a B piece. Press the seams toward the B pieces. Set-in the A/B section to make a unit. Make four of these units.

Unit two consists of sewing a D piece to a B piece. Press these seams toward the B piece. Make four of these units.

The third unit is the center section. Sew E pieces in units of two and press these seams in a circular fashion. Follow the instructions in Lesson 7 for the Eight-Pointed star. The center of the Castle Wall is like the center of an Eight-Pointed Star.

QUILTING IDEAS

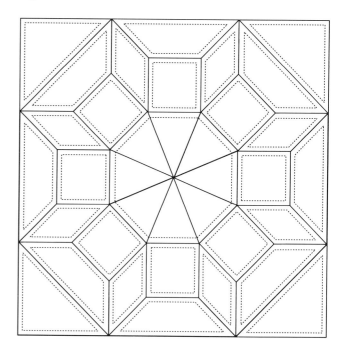

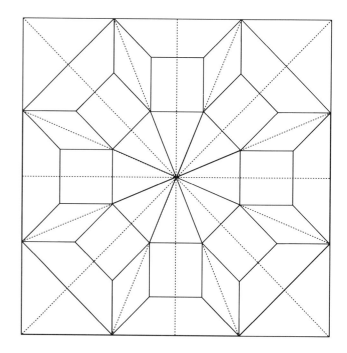

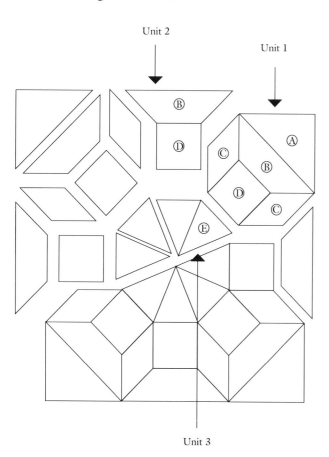

*Figure 13-3.*

# Lesson FOURTEEN

## Sand Dollar Design: Reverse Applique and Freezer Paper Turn-Under

*Figure 14-1.*

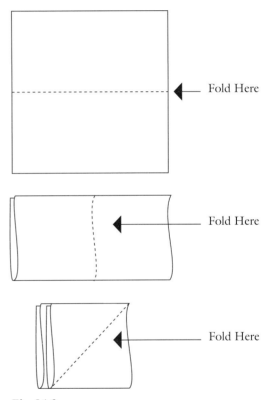

Fold Here

Fold Here

Fold Here

*Fig. 14-2.*

This pattern looks much harder than it really is. If you follow the directions on how to applique this piece, I think you will agree. The background area showing through the center circle and the leaf design are made by what is called reverse applique.

Cut a 12½" x 12½" square for the background fabric.

Cut a square that is 10" x 10" for the sand dollar design.

Fold the 10" square in half, in half again, and then fold one more time so the fabric is eight layers thick (Fig. 14-2).

Make a template for piece A (Fig. 14-3). Place the dotted lines on the folds of the fabric.

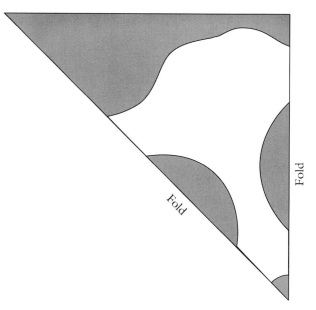

*Figure 14-4.*

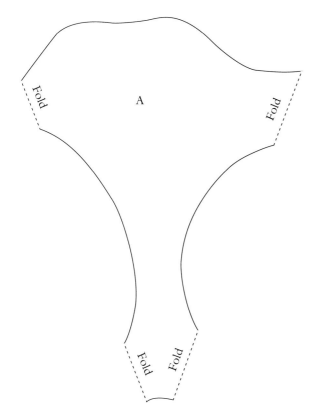

*Figure 14-3.*

Follow the directions for Lesson 5 for making the template. Trace the design onto the folded 10" square. Be sure the fold lines are on the folds of the fabric (Fig. 14-4). Cut the design adding a ¼" seam allowance. Do not forget the seam allowance. For the time being, only cut the outside edge. Unlike in Lesson 5, this design needs to have the seam allowance added.

Open the square and you will have your Sand Dollar design. It will look a little unusual because of the seam allowance.

Cut another Sand Dollar design from freezer paper. Fold the freezer-paper eight layers deep like the fabric. However, do not add a seam allowance to the freezer-paper template.

Center the freezer-paper template over the Sand Dollar design you cut from the fabric. Iron the freezer-paper template to the Sand Dollar design with a dry iron (Fig. 14-5).

Center the design on the background fabric. Secure the design to the background with glue or basting

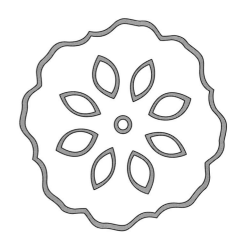

*Figure 14-5.*

stitches. Whatever your choice, stay at least ⅜" from the edges so as not to interfere with your turning under the seams.

Use the freezer paper as a guide to turn under the seam allowance. You will need to clip the inside curves and points to enable easier turning. Cut the reverse-applique areas away so that there is less than ¼" of seam allowance.

With the tip of your needle, turn under the seams. When you are finished, you will see only the background and the freezer paper. The Sand Dollar fabric will not show.

Remove the freezer-paper and press the folded Sand Dollar flat. The center section of the Sand Dollar section on this design is reverse applique. This is when you allow the background fabric to show through an opening.

## QUILTING IDEAS

# Section THREE

## Assembling the Quilt

When you have completed all of the individual blocks for your sampler, you will be ready to assemble them as a quilt. There are a few considerations and techniques you will need in order to accomplish that. Be sure to read through this section before beginning to assemble your quilt.

## SETTINGS

There are some different ways you can set the blocks for a sampler project.

One way is to build the blocks in rows, with all of the blocks being pieced or appliqued blocks. This could be done with the quilt-as-you-go method or making the whole top at one time and then quilting it later. A second way is to build the quilt in blocks, but with every other block being a solid or plain quilted square instead of a sampler block. Using this idea, you can either quilt the plain blocks with the same design or with all different designs. This can be done using either the quilt-as-you-go or the traditional method.

The next choice is whether to make the quilt with or without lattice. Most people prefer to make the sampler quilt with lattice to separate the blocks, but it can also be done without the lattice. Lattice can be used with the quilt-as-you-go and the regular methods.

Another choice is to build the quilt on the diagonal. This is best done when completing the top the traditional way, not using the quilt-as-you-go method, because of the corner and side triangles (Fig. 1).

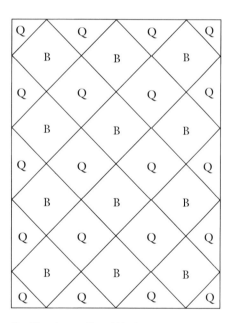

B = Pieced or appliqued blocks

Q = Quilted blocks

*Figure 1.*

## ASSEMBLY OF THE TOP

Let's discuss the assembly of these tops. This information was explained in Lesson 1, but will be reviewed again in this section. Using the quilt-as-you-go method, make your 12" block design. Add a 1½" lattice to the outside edges of your block. The lattice, or sashing, sets the blocks apart, framing each block. Attach strips to the sides first. They will be cut 12½" long. Then attach the top and bottom lattice strips. They will be cut 14½" long. The lattice fabric should be the same on all four sides and should stay the same on the rest of the blocks. Cut a square of batting and backing that is approximately 16". Layer the top, batting and backing, then baste the three layers together. I baste across the square on each diagonal and then around all four sides about ½" from the edges.

You are now ready to quilt this block. Place the square on a hoop or frame of your choice. The adjustable squares from Marie Products™ are nice because they can be adjusted to fit the square. If you are using a hoop, you will need to baste some extra fabric around the outside edges on all four sides of the piece so there is even tension on the piece during the quilting process. After all of your blocks are quilted, you are ready to attach the blocks together.

Lay the blocks out on the top of the bed or on the floor and decide which ones you want where. You do not want all of your darker squares in one row or all of the lighter squares in another row. Try to balance the squares by color. Stand away from the blocks and see if anything stands out or catches your eye. If so, it may need to be moved to another area. Once you have positioned everything, attach the blocks to each other in rows across. Place the blocks front to front. Pull the top layers of batting and backing away from the seam (Fig. 2). Then pull back the bottom layers of batting and backing. You only want the lattice fabric in the seam. Sew with a ¼" seam allowance, by hand or machine.

*Figure 2.*

The next step is to lay out a row of blocks, with the backs facing up. The batting in adjacent blocks will overlap. Lay one side of the batting flat and lay the other side of the batting on top of it (Fig. 3). I fold the batting in the even rows to one side, and the batting in the odd rows to the opposite side. This makes the seams stronger. Cut away any excess or overlapping of the batting. You only want *one* layer of batting in this area. If the batting overlaps, it will be twice as thick and it will be noticeable on the top of the quilt.

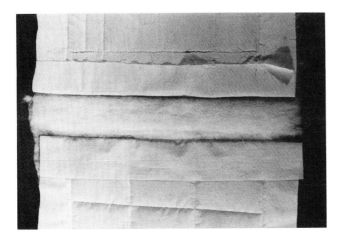

*Figure 3.*

Now fold the backing over. One side will overlap the other. Do not cut any of this away. I overlap it to one side and fold the raw edge under and blindstitch it closed. I use a single strand of sewing thread that matches the backing fabric. Use pins to hold the seam down while you do the sewing (Fig. 4). I fold all of these seams in one direction so the seams in each row will form a straight line down the back. You may not want to do any quilting in the lattice because of the thickness of the seams.

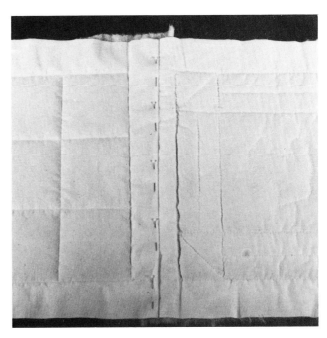

*Figure 4.*

When your rows are all done, attach row one to row two. Lay the fronts together; pin and sew the lattice strips. Lay this section flat and fold the batting in toward the seam area. Cut away any excess batting and fold the backing over. It will overlap. Fold the seam allowance under and blindstitch the seam closed.

After the blocks are assembled, you are ready to add the border. With this method, the first border strip must be the same as the lattice fabric. Cut four strips of lattice fabric 1½" wide and as long as the sides of your quilt. Sew these strips to the sides first and then to the top and bottom of the quilt. Now you are ready to add the border. Add the border closest to the inside of the quilt first. Attach the sides first and then the top and bottom. Sew these on to the outside lattice strip. Use as many borders as you want to finish your project. Press these seams away from the center. Be very careful not to iron the batting. Since it is made from a plastic, the hot iron will melt it.

Now, flip the quilt over onto the back. Add a strip of backing fabric that is as wide as all of the borders combined. Don't forget to add the seam allowance to these strips. If the borders total 15", cut a piece of fabric for the back that is 15½" wide. Sew these on the same as you did the borders on the front. Attach the sides first and then the top and bottom. Press these seams away from the center. You have the front and back borders made and attached. Simply place a piece of batting, the size of the borders, between the top and backing border fabrics and whipstitch it in place. I whipstitch the batting for the border to the batting that is already in the quilt squares. Then quilt the borders with a hoop or Q-Snap® frame. You will need to baste a scrap piece of fabric to the four outside edges so there is fabric inside the whole hoop area when you are quilting. You can quilt straight lines on the borders or purchase a nice border stencil from your local quilt shop.

If you want to put your top together the traditional way, piece all of your blocks first. Cut the lattice 2½", which includes the seam allowance. You can choose to use safe squares in the corners of each intersection (Fig. 5). Sew lattice in between the blocks first, building the horizontal rows. The lattice should be cut 2½" wide and 12½" long. After all the horizontal rows are attached, you are ready to attach the vertical lattice. If you are using safe squares, you can cut the lattice into 12½" sections and sew a square in between every lattice section. If you are not using safe squares, sew the long strips of lattice across the rows. Press the seams toward the lattice and away from the blocks. With this method, it is easier to do some quilting in the lattice because there are no seams. There are many good stencils available for quilting in this area.

Attach the border or borders. If you want to miter

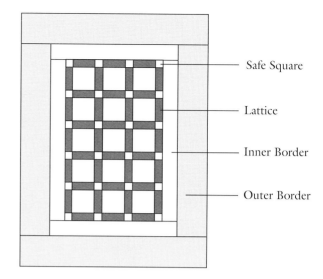

Figure 5.

the borders instead of using straight seams, it is very easy. I cut these borders a little longer than the finished size needs to be so I have room to work with the miters. Cut the border strips, adding the seam allowance. For this sample, let's say we have an inside and an outside border. Sew the inside border to the outside border. Do this four times for the two sides and the top and the bottom. Center the complete border on top of the quilt edges and pin in place. Sew from the ¼" seam to the ¼" seam, not raw edge to raw edge. Do this for the sides, the top and the bottom. Now, choose a corner and lay the two borders that meet in the corner on top of each other, front to front. You are now ready to miter the corners (Fig. 6).

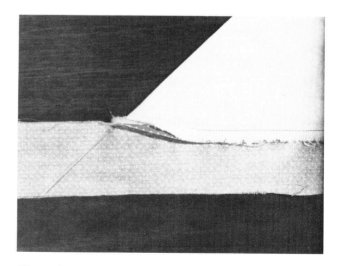

Figure 6.

With a ruler, place the 45° angle on the outside raw edge of the fabric. The long side of the ruler must line up with the ¼" seam where you stopped and started to quilt. Draw the line down the long side of the ruler from the ¼" seam to the outside raw edge (Fig. 7).

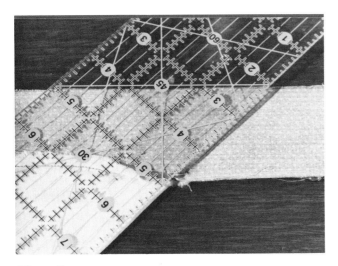

*Figure 7.*

Place some pins on this line so it does not shift when you take it to the sewing machine. Sew on this line from the inside to the outside; remove the pins as you get to them. Press the seam to one side or the other. Do this before cutting any excess from the back of the miter. If the miter has a pucker at the corner of the blocks, it is usually a simple problem to solve. Check where you started to sew. This problem is usually caused by starting outside the ¼". Simply remove some of the beginning stitches and start again and be sure to start right on the ¼" mark. Press these seams to one side and cut away any excess.

You will now need to baste the three layers together. Place the backing flat on the floor. If working on the carpet, I pin the backing to the carpet, with the right side of the fabric down. I pin the corners and use three to four pins on each side. This prevents shifting when the batting is opened and placed on the top of the backing. Center the batting over the backing and be sure both are flat. Now place the quilt top, right side up, on top of the batting, making sure it is flat. Baste the three layers together. Baste in lines 8 to 10 inches apart if the quilt is going in a large floor frame, 6" apart if you will be using a hoop or small frame.

More basting is done if you are working in a hoop because it will be moved more and the basting prevents shifting. Remember to quilt from the center to the outside edges.

## BATTINGS

The thinnest of the polyester battings is the best kind to use when you are starting to quilt because it will give you the smallest stitches.

The thickest battings, sometimes referred to as fat or high batts, are not recommended for quilting. They are best for tying and will give a comforter type look. They are too thick for small quilting stitches.

The medium-thickness battings come in polyester, cotton, cotton blends and wool. The medium-thickness polyester is recommended for quilting when seeking a puffier look. Keep in mind you will not be able to keep your stitches as small with these batts as with the thinner batting.

There is a batting of 80% cotton and 20% polyester. I have found this batting to be difficult to hand quilt. It does have shrinkage. The company recommends that the batting be prewashed if you are going to use it in a quilt. It is recommended that you quilt no more than 2" apart to prevent shifting of the batting when it is washed. If you are considering machine quilting at some time, I would suggest you try this batting. If you do not prewash the batting and you allow shrinkage to take place after washing, it will give more of an antique look. If you are interested in machine quilting, I highly recommend Harriet Hargrave's book called *Heirloom Machine Quilting*, and Lois Smith's book, *Fun and Fancy Machine Quiltmaking*. These books are excellent and explain machine quilting in detail.

There is also a needle-punched 100% polyester batting. This batting is also more difficult to hand quilt because of its density.

The next choice of batting is 100% cotton. Of the different brands of 100% cotton, I prefer Mountain Mist Blue Ribbon® because it does not require prewashing and only needs to be quilted every two inches. Other brands require prewashing and need to be quilted every inch. The advantages of 100% cotton batting are that it has a longer life expectancy and its natural fibers will breathe, keeping you cool in the summer and warm in the winter. The disadvantage is that it does require more quilting. It is also more difficult to quilt in the summer because the cotton draws moisture. This causes the needle to stick as it passes through the batting, making it difficult to pull the needle through the batting.

In the medium-weight category there is a 100% wool batting. Like cotton, wool is a natural fiber and has many of the same tendencies. It is wonderful to quilt. Your needle glides easily through the batting, which enables you to keep stitches small. Heartfelt™, a leading supplier of wool batts, recommends you steam the batting with your iron before quilting. Every bag has a brochure that recommends how to use and care for the batting. The disadvantages are that it must be quilted closely, must be washed in the bathtub to avoid shrinkage and it must be air dried. It is also five to six times as expensive as cotton or polyester. Before you try wool, read the label. Some wool battings need to be wrapped in cheese cloth to minimize bearding. Bearding occurs when the batting fibers migrate through the fabric.

Be aware that battings do come in different sizes and you must buy the size you need for your project. Sizes range from crib size to king size.

# QUILTING

## MARKING THE QUILTING DESIGN

Depending on the type of marker you use, the quilting lines can be marked before or after the piece is basted. For example, if you are using chalk, it is better to wait until after the piece is basted so the lines do not brush off before you are ready to quilt. If you are using a silver or white pencil, you may find it easier to mark the lines before the piece is basted. Blue markers and ¼" tape can be used either before or after basting.

If you are marking on a dark fabric, you may find this method useful: trace the design you want to quilt onto a piece of paper. With a large needle or with your sewing machine, punch holes through the paper following the design. Place some cornstarch in a small piece of

muslin and tie it inside with some string. The cornstarch forms a little ball at the bottom. Place the paper design over the fabric you are marking. Lightly pound the cornstarch on the design. Lift the paper and use a white or silver pencil to connect the dots.

Another good way to mark dark fabric is by using white Saral® paper. Saral® paper can be purchased at art supply stores. Place fabric to be marked flat, paper with the chalk side down on the fabric and the quilting design on top of the paper. Trace over the design and it will transfer to the darker fabric.

You can use a light box under lighter fabrics. Since light boxes can be expensive, I use my kitchen table. Remove the center leaf and place a smooth edged piece of glass over the opening. Place a lamp, with the shade removed, under the table and you have created your own light box. Place the design to be quilted over the glass. Place the fabric over the design and trace.

There are several different sources for quilting designs. You can purchase stencils which are pre-cut designs to fit an area. Stencils are made of plastic and the designs are limitless. Each stencil indicates the area it will fit. If for some reason it does not, take a measurement to ensure that it will fit the needed area.

Cookie cutters are another source of quilting designs. They are simple and fun. Children's coloring books also have some excellent ideas for quilt patterns. They are interesting, yet have simple lines. (Cookie cutters and children's coloring books are also good sources for applique designs.)

## MAKING THE QUILTING STITCH

Use thread that is recommended for quilting. It is heavier than regular sewing thread. Cut the thread approximately 18" long. If it is too long, it will keep knotting. You will need to use your thimble, placed on the middle finger of your dominant hand. It should fit comfortably.

Tie a single knot at the end of your thread. Bring the needle in through only the top fabric and a little of the batting, about one needle's length from where you plan to start quilting. Bring the point of the needle out of the top fabric at the exact spot where you want to start quilting. Tug lightly on the thread and the knot should pop into the middle layer, which is the batting. The reason for coming in a needle's length away is to keep the knot away from the point where you started quilting. This helps to prevent the knot from popping out when the quilt is laundered and used.

The quilting stitch is a running stitch. Proceed to do a running stitch through all three layers. You should use a rocking motion; there should be two to three stitches on the needle at a time (Fig. 8). Use the thimble to push the needle. The thumb on your dominant hand should be out front. Push down with your thumb while pushing up from the bottom with your finger. This helps to get better leverage and keeps the stitches smaller. Be patient as you're learning.

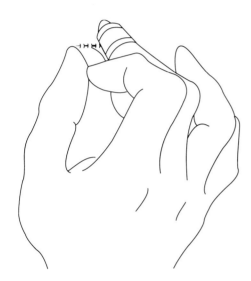

*Figure 8.*

The bottom finger also does some of the work (Fig. 9). Use this finger to push up on the needle. As soon as the needle touches your bottom finger, push up and allow the needle to roll off of your finger or fingernail. You need to feel the needle to ensure that you are through all three layers.

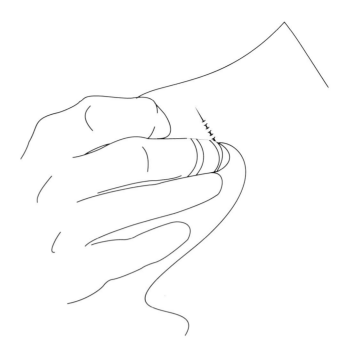

*Figure 9.*

If your bottom finger gets sore, there are some things you can try. On the tip of your finger, put either clear nail polish or a product called Second Skin®. Either will protect the skin yet still allow you to feel the needle.

Most quilters find it easier to quilt in certain directions. I prefer top to bottom and right to left. For you, it may be two different directions. The most important thing to remember when you are first starting to quilt is to keep the quilting stitches straight and even. Once you have accomplished this, concentrate on getting the stitches smaller. The average number of stitches is eight to the inch. This means eight on the top and eight on the bottom.

## TRAVELING BETWEEN DESIGN AREAS AND ENDING LINES OF QUILTING

If you find that you still have enough thread on your needle at the end of a section, and want to move to another section, you can travel through the batting to another section. Run the needle through the batting and bring it up at the area where you want to start quilting. Be sure you do not come out the back of the quilt. You can travel two to three needle lengths if necessary. This is done by taking the needle into the batting, bringing the front of the needle out, keeping the back of the needle in the fabric, pivoting the back and pushing the point of the needle with your fingernail, pivoting the front and pull the needle out where you want to start quilting. Do not travel through the fabric if you can see the thread through the surface. This happens with some lighter-colored fabrics.

I also use a form of traveling when I stop quilting. At the end of a line of quilting you can tie a knot in the thread close to the surface of the quilt. Then insert the needle into the quilt and pull the knot through the surface and into the batting. But I backtrack and crisscross the stitches from where I just came, to anchor the thread.

When finishing, I sew my stitches in this manner:

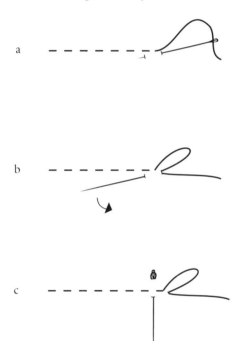

Figure 10.

Step 1. Insert the needle into the fabric at the end of the line of quilting, as though you were taking a last stitch in the line. Go into and through the batting, but do not come out through the backing fabric. Instead, make a stitch in the batting only by moving the needle forward slightly and then angling your needle to come back through the batting and through the top to the surface of the quilt. Your needle will emerge as shown in Fig. 10a.

Step 2. Pull the needle through until its eye is no longer visible because it is between the top and the batting. Don't pull any more. With the eye of the needle still under the surface of the fabric, use the pointed end of the needle as a "handle" and pivot your needle so the eye is positioned to cross under your line of quilting (Fig. 10b). Still using the pointed end of your needle as a "handle," push the eye end of the needle through the fabric of the top (Fig. 10c), being careful not to pull any threads in the fabric.

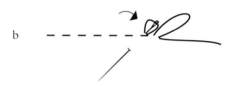

Figure 11.

Step 3. Once the eye has come through the top, grasp it and pull it through far enough to bring the point of the needle underneath the line of quilting and to the other side of it, as shown in Fig. 11a. (The point will still be underneath the top of the quilt, but you will be able to feel its location.) Now, use the eye end as a handle and pivot the needle as shown in Fig. 11b, so you can take a last diagonal stitch beneath your line of quilting and then bring the point of the needle through the surface of the quilt top.

Step 4. Once you have brought the needle through to the surface, pull it to tighten the last stitch in your line of quilting, and the crossing stitches you have made to secure your thread. Then clip the thread off at the surface of your quilt, and your line of quilting is not fully secured. Some people find this easy to remember as an "S" shape or zigzag forming under the line of quilting.

Proper lighting will help you make your stitches small and consistent. Try to work with the light over your shoulder and toward the direction you are quilt-

frame, have the light directly across from you or directly over you, creating no shadows. Use the highest wattage bulb recommended for your light. You may want to remove the shade from your lamp if it does not seem bright enough.

The first stitch in a line of quilting is always the hardest. Keep working at making it consistent and it will eventually be the same size as the rest of your stitches. To keep the first stitch as small as the other stitches, take the stitch quickly. Do not spend a lot of time thinking about it. When you are working in a hoop or small frame, always start from the center and work to the outside edges of your piece. When working in a floor frame, quilt from one side to the opposite side or from the top to the bottom.

As you are quilting, it is safe to remove the basting stitches from those areas already quilted.

## ADDING BINDING

Your project is nearly complete. The final step is binding the edges of the quilt or wallhanging. Trim the batting and backing even with the top. The binding is placed on the outside raw edges to finish with a nice, even edge. If the project you are making is going to get a lot of use, it should have bias binding on the outside edges. If it is going to be hung on the wall, you may use grain-line binding. The reason for using bias binding on something that will get a lot of use is that it has some give and will wear better and longer. Never use purchased binding. The quality of the fabric in purchased binding is not as good as the cotton fabric you use for quilting, and it is never easy to match the exact color of the purchased binding to the color in the quilt. It is simple to make your own binding.

### GRAIN-LINE BINDING

First, let's start with grain-line binding for those projects that are not going to get a lot of wear. Cut strips of fabric on the grain line that are two inches wide. Make sure you cut enough fabric to go around your project. Measure all four sides of your project and add 10" for seams and corners.

Sew the ends of these strips together, right sides facing each other, and press the seams open. You should now have one long strip of binding. You now have two choices: French binding or regular binding. French binding is made when you fold the binding in half and press it. Regular binding is run through a bias tape maker. Your finished product will look like store-packaged binding.

As mentioned earlier, I like to use the bias maker from Clover™. Feed the binding through the larger end. There is a slit on the top of the bias maker, so if your binding does not want to go through, you can push it through with a pin. Place the bias maker on your ironing board and iron the folds as they come out the other end of the bias maker. The bias maker folds the two sides over evenly. Keep your iron flat on the board and pull the binding out the other side of the iron. The bias maker has a little handle to hold on to. This tool is a great time-saving device. The first time I made binding, I ironed the folds by hand without the use of the bias maker. It took hours. The bias maker allows you to make binding in about 15 minutes. You can use it with either bias binding or grain-line binding (Fig. 12).

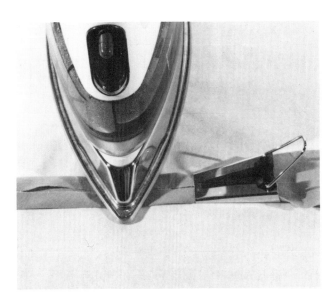

*Figure 12.*

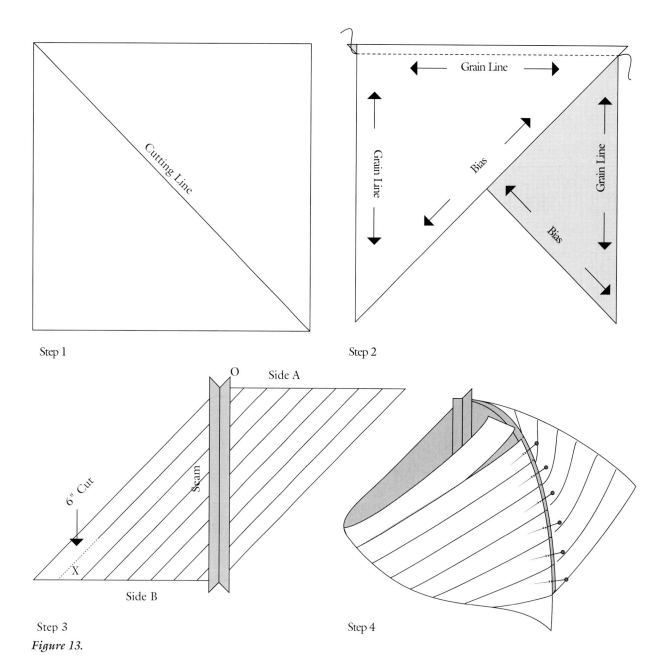

Step 1

Step 2

Step 3

Step 4

*Figure 13.*

## BIAS BINDING

Bias binding is also easy to make. Using measurements from the yardage chart (pg. 25), cut the largest possible square. Then, proceed as shown in Fig. 13. Fold the large square in half and cut it into two triangles (Step 1). Place these two triangles together front-to-front, as shown in Step 2. Sew with a ¼" seam allowance. When you open the triangles, they will form a parallelogram. Use your ruler and mark the entire back side of the parallelogram with lines spaced 2" apart (Step 3). Cut into the first 2" line about six inches. Connect X to O and side A to side B to form a tube.

Use pins to line up the 2" lines at the seam (Step 4). Sew this seam with a ¼" seam allowance. You will notice that there is an extra two-inch piece of fabric at each end. This is correct because you started 2 inches over. Continue to cut on the line where you started.

Place your tube on the ironing board so you can keep cutting and not have to worry about cutting the wrong portion of the tube behind it. When you are finished cutting, you will have one long continuous piece of bias binding. You can then fold this with the binding maker or make French binding.

You are now ready to attach the bias to the quilt.

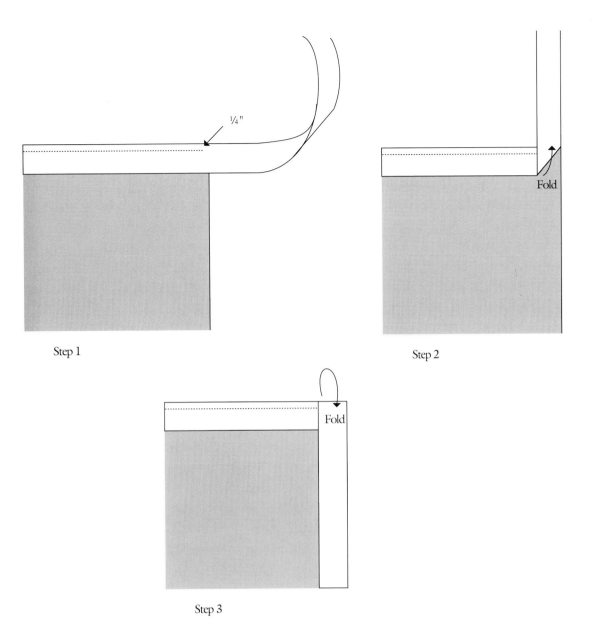

Step 1

Step 2

Step 3

*Figure 14.*

For French binding, place the binding on top of the quilt with the raw edges facing out and the folded edge facing in toward the quilt.

Do not start on a corner; start on a side, or the top or bottom. As you start, fold the end of the binding strip in about ¼," so you do not have a raw edge. Use your sewing machine and sew with a ¼" seam allowance until you reach the first corner. Stop ¼" away from the corner (Fig. 14, Step 1). Take a back stitch to secure the binding. Remove the quilt from the sewing machine.

Fold the binding straight up as in the diagram, keeping the fold in place (Step 2). Then fold the binding down so it is now even with the edge of the quilt (Step

3). Place your project back in the sewing machine and again sew with a ¼" seam allowance. Do all four corners like this and you will have formed a little miter in the corner. Overlap the ends and then hand stitch the miters on the closed corners.

After the top portion is machine sewn in place, the binding is folded over the raw edges of the backing, batting and quilt top. Pin the binding in position on the back. Hand stitch the fold of the binding with a blind or applique stitch.

If you made regular binding, open the one fold and place the raw edge of that fold on the edge of the quilt and the folded side will be in toward the center of the quilt. Sew along the fold at that edge of the binding, and proceed as for French binding.

## CARING FOR YOUR FINISHED PIECE

If you need to store a quilted item for any extended period of time, it should be placed in a pillowcase. Never store quilts in plastic. Plastic can draw moisture and stain the quilt. If it is necessary to fold the piece, consider putting something in the folds to prevent creases. A good choice is muslin or acid-free tissue.

If you have the room, a larger quilt can be placed in white sheets and rolled on plastic PVC pipe for storage.

Never expose a finished piece to direct sunlight. The sun will very quickly fade the fabric.

## CLEANING YOUR QUILT

I wash almost all of my work by hand, using Orvus® and working in the washing machine's tub. Put one tablespoon in the machine and allow it to dissolve. Then place the quilted piece in the water and, with your hands, gently swish the quilted item around. The machine must not be allowed to agitate. Rinse several times until the water is clear. To remove the excess water, place the item in the machine on spin only.

Next, place the project between two sheets and either place it on the lawn to dry or on top of some flat shrubs. Another good thing to place the quilt on or in between are old, clean mattress pads. This allows air to circulate and dry the piece within one to two hours. If the project is larger, place it between sheets on the grass and weight the corners with stones to keep the wind from blowing the top sheet off of the quilt. Sunlight will cause the fabric to fade. Turn the quilt after the first hour to allow the air to dry it faster. Agitation in the washer and the bouncing in the dryer are too hard on the fabrics and hand work to take any chances.

Never dry clean your quilts. The chemical dry-cleaning process can fade the fabrics.

If you only need to remove dust, use your vacuum to suck the dust from the surface. Keep the vacuum on low power and use a soft brush attachment. Better yet, use a protective screen between the fabric and the vacuum.

If your quilt is being given as a gift, it is a good idea to sew a label on the back with the proper washing directions. It is also not a bad idea to give the receiver the washing soap you are recommending so it will be easy for them to care for the quilt.

## HANGING YOUR QUILT

If you are planning to hang a finished piece, sew a sleeve on the top back of the project. Use the same fabric for the sleeve that you used for the backing. Cut the piece for the tube 8" wide and 4" shorter than the finished piece. Sew the length together and turn the tube inside out. Iron the tube flat. Applique the tube to the top of the wallhanging. Leave the ends open.

At the hardware store, buy a dowel or a 1 x 3 that is 1" shorter than your quilt. While at the hardware store, buy eye screws. They are shaped like a screw at one end with a loop on the top. Place one of these screws upright at both ends of the dowel. Also, buy finishing nails. They do not have a head so they will go through the eye of the screw. Hold the dowel to the wall and center it. Use a pencil and mark through the center of the eye screws, making small dots on the wall. Now, hammer in the two finishing nails at those two dots. Slide the dowel between the two layers of the sleeve and secure the eye screws on the nails.

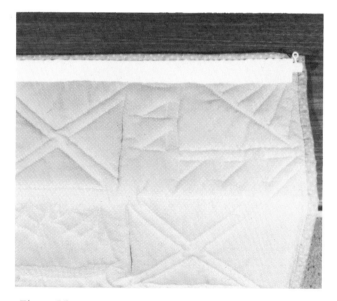

*Figure 15.*

# MAKING BLOCKS
# INTO PILLOWS

If you want to make a pillow or pillows to match your quilt, here are basic instructions.

Make a 12" square from one of the designs in this book. Add a 2" lattice around all four sides. Press lattice seams away from the center. Baste the three layers and quilt the block. Cut a piece of fabric to be used for the back of the pillow. It should be cut the same size as the square you have made for the top. If you are not going to use a ruffle, piping or lace, you will simply sew the pillow front to the pillow back. Pin the front to the back, right sides together. Sew around the four sides, leaving approximately a 6" opening for turning. Leave the opening in the middle of one of the sides or the bottom. Before you turn the pillow, clip the four corners to remove excess fabric and to help make a sharper point on the corners. After the pillow is turned, I use a pencil point in the inside to push out the four corners.

After the pillow is stuffed, hand stitch the opening closed with two strands of matching sewing thread. You could also put a zipper in this opening. Just leave a space big enough for the size zipper you choose. If you do not know how to work with a zipper or prefer not to, you can make the back of the pillow with an opening so the pillow form can be placed inside. This requires cutting two pieces of fabric for the back. If the pillow is a 16" square, cut two pieces of backing 16½" x 12". On one 12" side of each of the backing pieces, fold the raw edge under ½" and sew with a top stitch. Fold the edge under once more and top stitch again. This is to keep the raw edge covered. Overlap the two backing pieces until they form a 16" square. Baste these together. You can use Velcro® or snaps to hold this opening closed after you have stuffed the pillow. Now you are ready to attach the pillow front and back.

There are ready-made pillow forms that come in several different sizes. If one of these will fit, you do not need to make your own. I prefer to make my own case for the stuffing. I take two square pieces of muslin the size of the pillow. Sew these together, leaving an opening of approximately 6". Stuff the case and sew the opening closed. Place it in the pillow.

If you are adding piping, pre-gathered lace or a ruffle, you will need to do this before the top and back are sewn together. Take the trim and place it with the raw edge over the raw edge of the pillow, right sides together, and the trim facing in toward the center of the square. Baste the trim to the top of the pillow. Do not begin the trim on a corner; start on one of the sides. Allow extra trim at the corners for turning. Overlap the trim when ending. Now you are ready to attach the back. Sew the front and back together, right sides facing. Then turn right side out using the zipper or other opening on the back.

# AFTERWORD

I hope you have enjoyed your quilting experience. After you have made the blocks in the lessons, you are ready to tackle any project. Just take it one step at a time. There are numerous patterns in the last section of this book. They all appear some place in the color portion of the book.

As with anything in life, the more you do it the better your results. Do not stop here. Keep going. There are many great books and teachers. You have only just begun. The possibilities are endless. Each new project will bring you new ideas and greater skill. Good luck and remember, KEEP QUILTING!

# SOURCES

• Pat Andreatta (Bias Bars® and applique books) 626 Shadowood Lane, Warren, OH, 44484

• Airwick Industries, Inc, (Easy Wash™), Carlstadt, NJ, 07072

• Clover™ (binding maker and chalk wheels), 1007 E. Dominguez, Suite N, Carson, CA, 90746

• Heartfelt™ (wool batting), RFD 340, Vineyard Haven, MA, 02768

• House of Quilting (paddle thimbles), Route 3, Box 433, Fayetteville, NC, 28306

• Lamb Art Press™, (Q-Snap frames®), P.O. Box 38, Parsons, TN, 38363

• Marie Products™ (hoops and frames), P.O. Box 56000, Tucson, AZ, 85703

• Proctor and Gamble (Orvus™), Cincinnati, OH, 45215

•Sterns, The (batting and Ensure™), Mountain Mist Products®, 100 Williams St., Cincinnati, OH, 45215

• Wallflower Designs™ (Pigma™ pens and labels), 1573 Millersville RD, Millersville, MD, 21108

• Check your area for quilting magazines. They list many sources for quilting supplies.

Patterns for most of the blocks shown in the sampler quilt photographs are included in the book. If a pattern is not given for the block you would like to make, send a self-addressed, stamped envelope and $1 to: Karen Buckley, 1237 Holly Pike, Carlisle, PA 17013.

# BIBLIOGRAPHY

Cohen, Allen C., *Beyond Basic Textiles*, Fairchild Publications, New York, New York, 1982.

Hargrave, Harriet; *Heirloom Machine Quilting*, Martinez, CA. 1990.

Pizzuto, Joseph J.; *Fabric Science*, Fairchild Publications, New York, New York, 1987.

Simms, Ami; *How to Improve Your Quilting Stitch*, Flint, Michigan, 1987.

# Section Four

## Full-Size Patterns for 12" Blocks

After you have completed the lessons in this book, the following patterns will seem easy. Enjoy adding these to your sampler quilt.

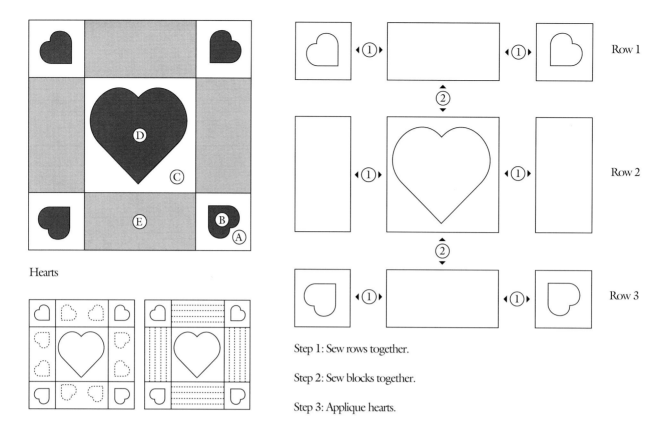

Hearts

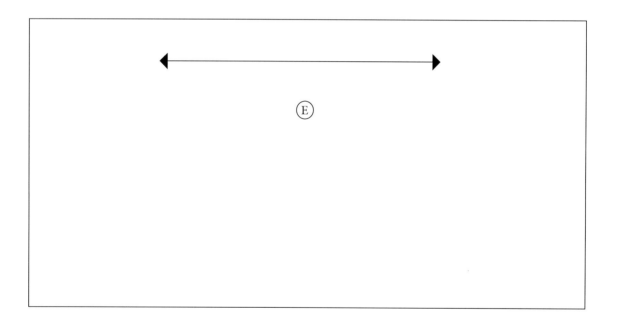

Quilting Ideas

Row 1

Row 2

Row 3

Step 1: Sew rows together.

Step 2: Sew blocks together.

Step 3: Applique hearts.

Ⓔ

A – Cut 4

B – Cut 4

C – Cut 1

D – Cut 1

E – Cut 4

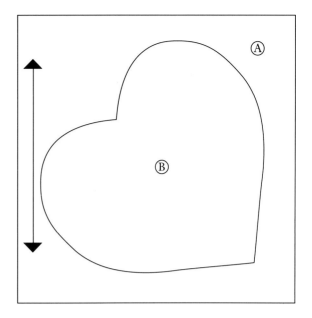

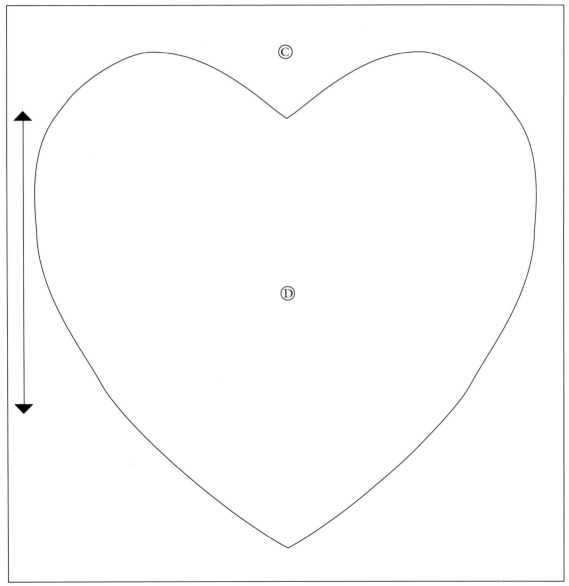

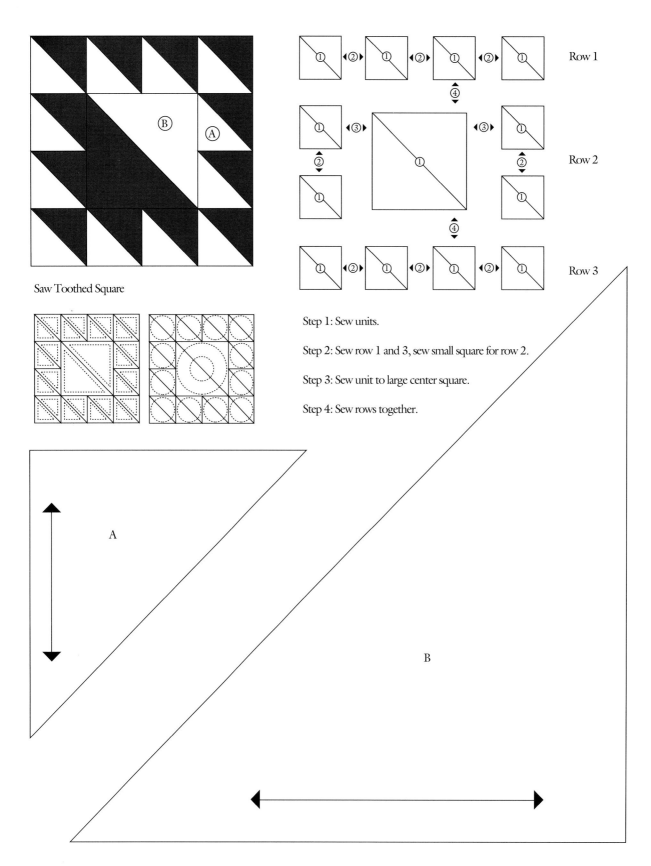

Saw Toothed Square

Row 1

Row 2

Row 3

Step 1: Sew units.

Step 2: Sew row 1 and 3, sew small square for row 2.

Step 3: Sew unit to large center square.

Step 4: Sew rows together.

A

B

A – Cut 24

B – Cut 2

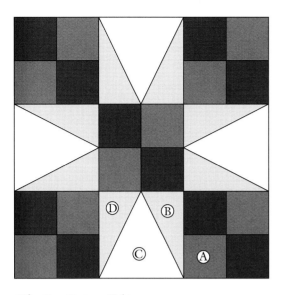

Fifty –Four Forty, or Fight

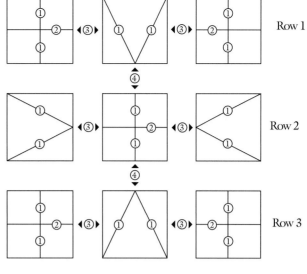

Row 1

Row 2

Row 3

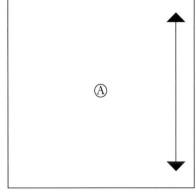

Quilting Ideas

Step 1: Sew units.

Step 2: Finish units.

Step 3: Sew rows together.

Step 4: Finish block.

A – Cut 20
B – Cut 4
C – Cut 4
D – Cut 4

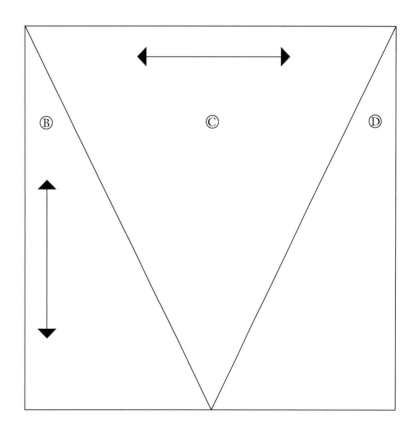

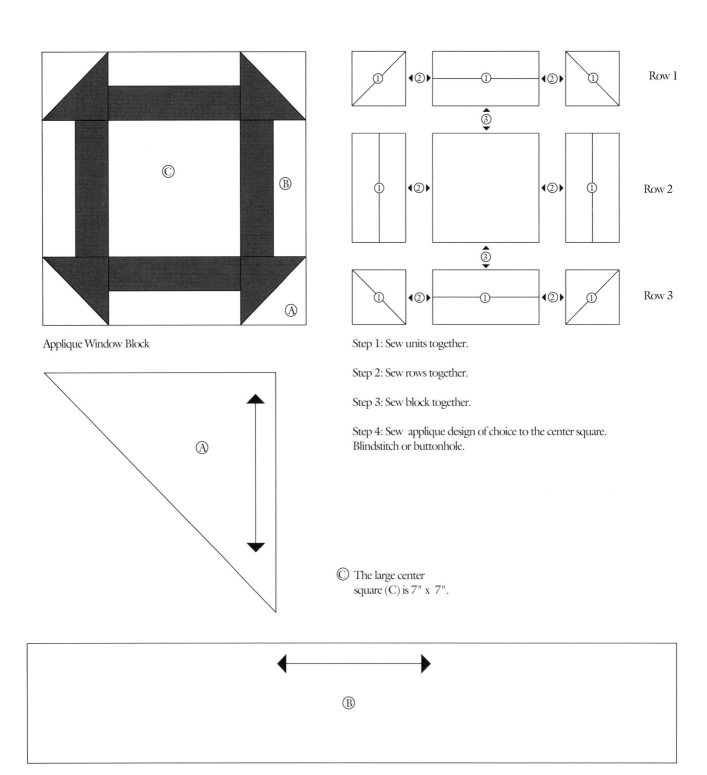

Applique Window Block

Step 1: Sew units together.

Step 2: Sew rows together.

Step 3: Sew block together.

Step 4: Sew applique design of choice to the center square. Blindstitch or buttonhole.

Ⓒ The large center square (C) is 7" x 7".

A – Cut 8

B – Cut 8

C – Cut 1

Choose either of the two designs on page 113 for the center of this block.

Dotted line indicates area to overlap.

113

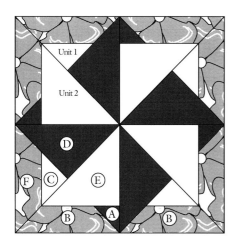

Spinning Wheel

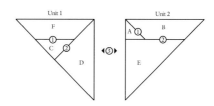

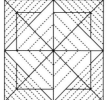

Quilting Ideas

Unit 1 – Step 1: Sew C to F.
Step 2: Sew step 1 to D.

Unit 2 – Step 1: Sew A to B.
Step 2: Sew step 1 to E.

Make four of Unit 1 and four of Unit 2.

Step 3 : Sew all units together.

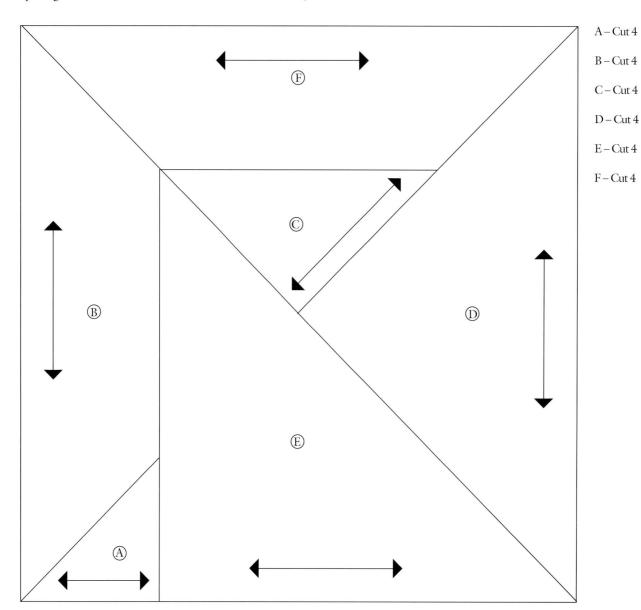

A – Cut 4

B – Cut 4

C – Cut 4

D – Cut 4

E – Cut 4

F – Cut 4

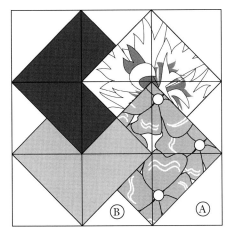

Card Tricks

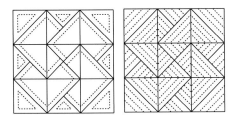

Quilting Ideas

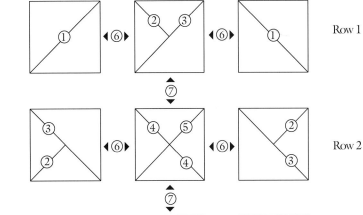
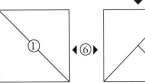

Row 1

Row 2

Row 3

Step 1: Sew 4 corners.

Step 2: Sew triangles.

Step 3: Set step 2 to above.

Step 4: Sew 2 triangles.

Step 5: Sew step 1 together.

Step 6: Sew rows together.

Step 7: Complete block.

A – Cut 12

B – Cut 12

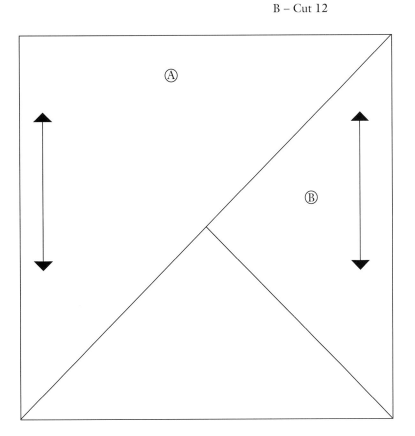

Double Ax or Spools

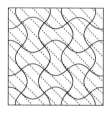

Quilting Ideas

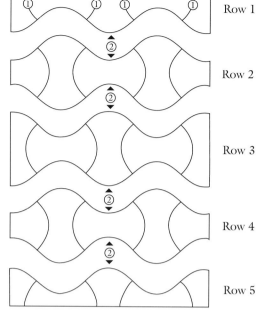

Row 1

Row 2

Row 3

Row 4

Row 5

Step 1: Sew spools into rows.

Step 2: Sew rows together.

Use full-size spools and then cut into a 12½" square. You will need to cut 25 spools.

The larger template is the cutting line template.
The smaller template is to be placed inside the larger template.
You will then draw around the smaller template to make your sewing lines.

A – Cut 25

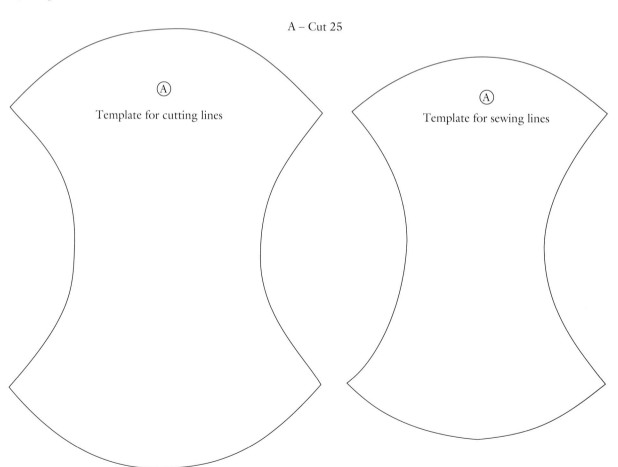

Ⓐ
Template for cutting lines

Ⓐ
Template for sewing lines

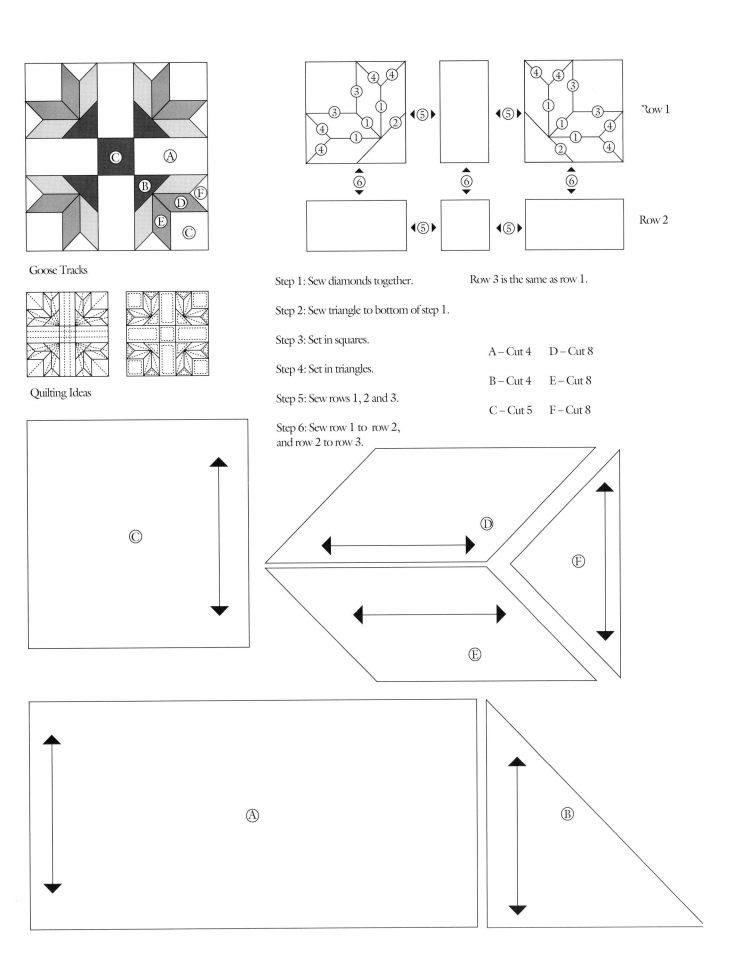

Goose Tracks

Quilting Ideas

Step 1: Sew diamonds together.

Step 2: Sew triangle to bottom of step 1.

Step 3: Set in squares.

Step 4: Set in triangles.

Step 5: Sew rows 1, 2 and 3.

Step 6: Sew row 1 to row 2, and row 2 to row 3.

Row 3 is the same as row 1.

A – Cut 4     D – Cut 8

B – Cut 4     E – Cut 8

C – Cut 5     F – Cut 8

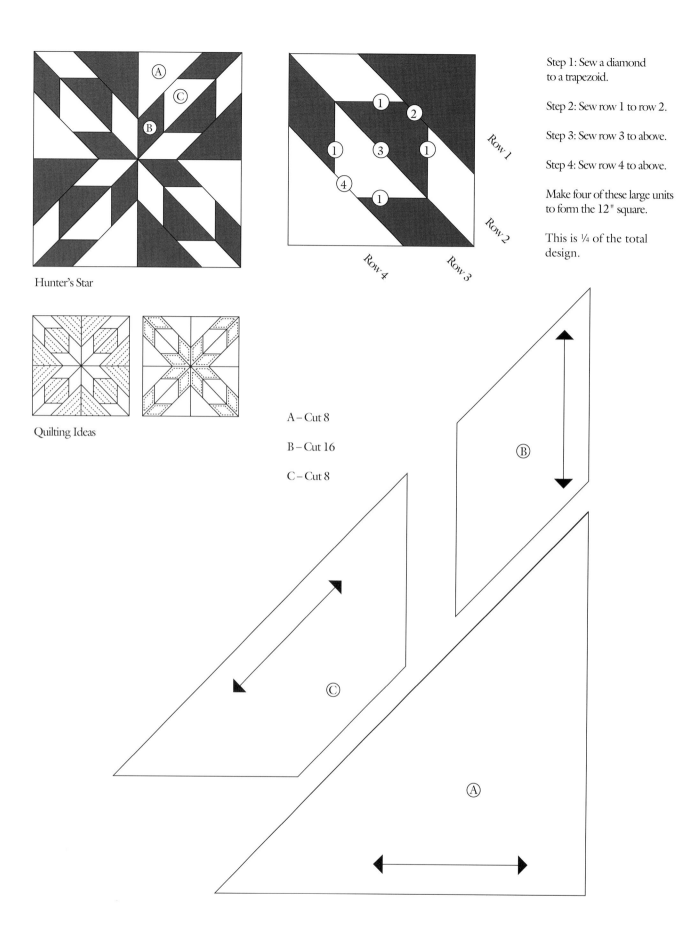

Hunter's Star

Quilting Ideas

Step 1: Sew a diamond to a trapezoid.

Step 2: Sew row 1 to row 2.

Step 3: Sew row 3 to above.

Step 4: Sew row 4 to above.

Make four of these large units to form the 12" square.

This is ¼ of the total design.

Row 1

Row 2

Row 3

Row 4

A – Cut 8

B – Cut 16

C – Cut 8

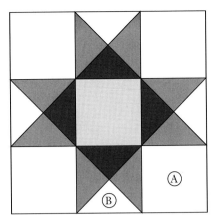

Ohio Star

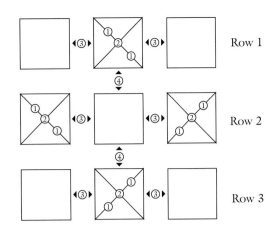

Row 1

Row 2

Row 3

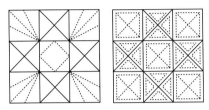

Quilting Ideas

Step 1: Sew triangles together.

Step 2: Sew step one into unit.

Step 3: Sew rows together.

Step 4: Sew block together.

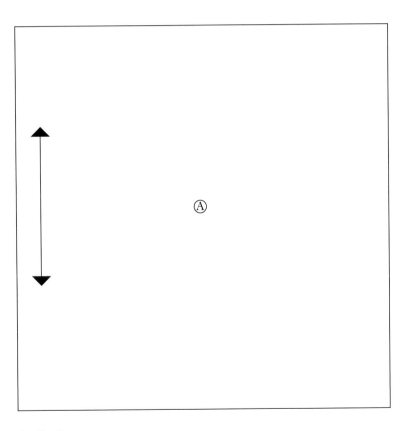

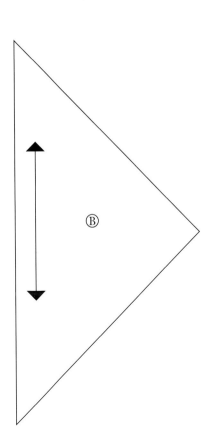

A – Cut 5

B – Cut 16

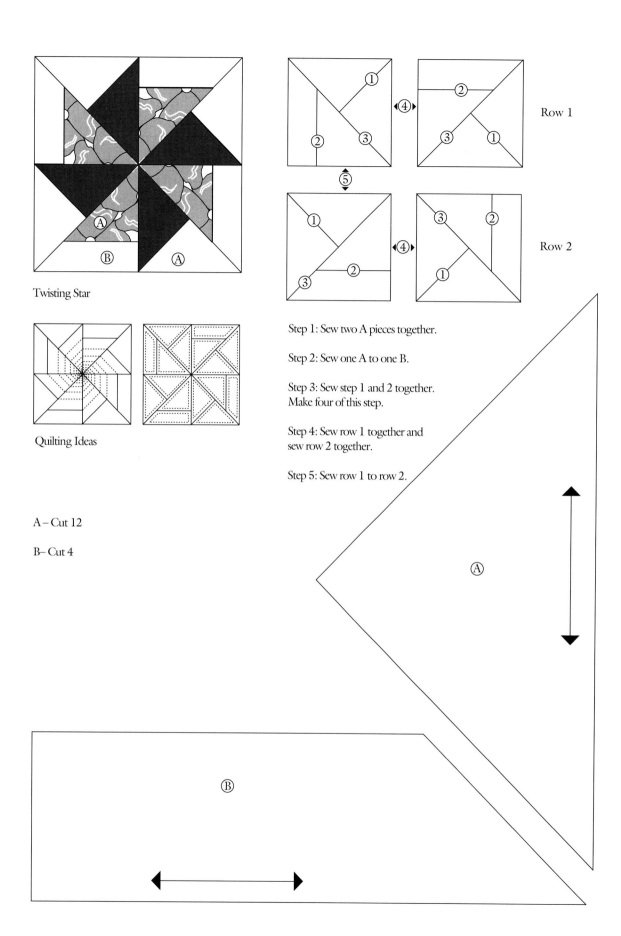

Twisting Star

Quilting Ideas

Step 1: Sew two A pieces together.

Step 2: Sew one A to one B.

Step 3: Sew step 1 and 2 together.
Make four of this step.

Step 4: Sew row 1 together and
sew row 2 together.

Step 5: Sew row 1 to row 2.

Row 1

Row 2

A – Cut 12

B – Cut 4

Ⓐ

Ⓑ

  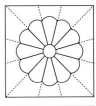 

Dresden Plate                                                                                    Quilting Ideas

Cut a 12½" x 12½" background square.
If you are doing the 9" plate, cut 12 sections. If you are doing the 11" plate, cut 20 sections.
You can cut a circle for the center to let the background show through.
Sew the sections in units of two. Sew from the outside to the inside. Then sew the units to form the circle.
Press all seams in one direction.
Center and pin the plate design to the background. Applique the Quilting ideas.

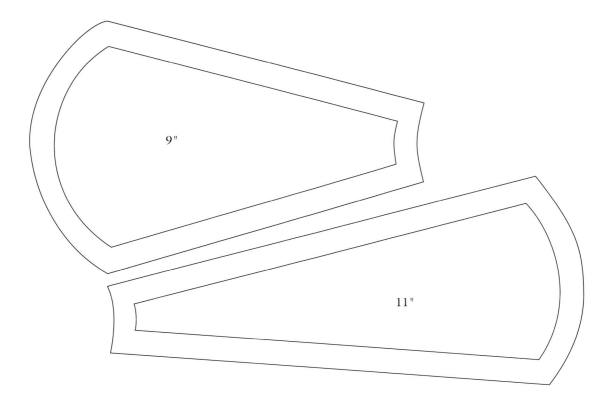

9"

11"

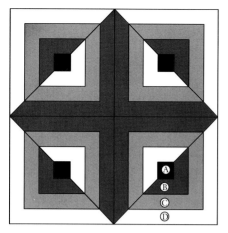

Log Cabin Variation

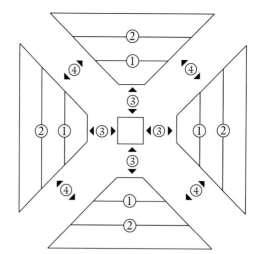

Step 1: Sew small trapezoid to middle trapezoid.

Step 2: Sew large trapezoid to step 1.

Step 3: Sew each section 2 to center square.

Step 4: Sew mitered seams.

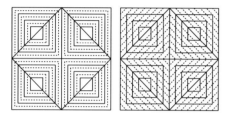

Quilting Ideas

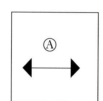

A – Cut 4

B – Cut 16

C – Cut 16

D – Cut 16

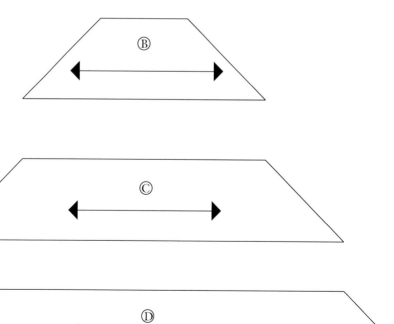

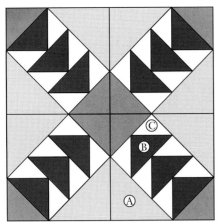

Geese in Flight

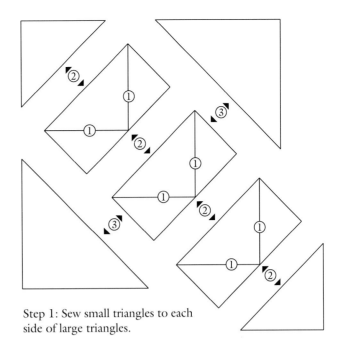

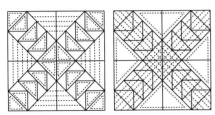

Quilting Ideas

Step 1: Sew small triangles to each side of large triangles.

Step 2: Sew units from step 1 and end triangles together.

Step 3: Sew large outer triangles to previous section.

Make three more of this unit and sew them together.

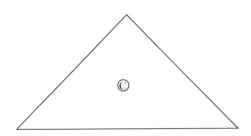

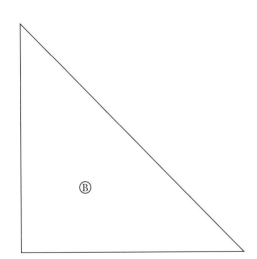

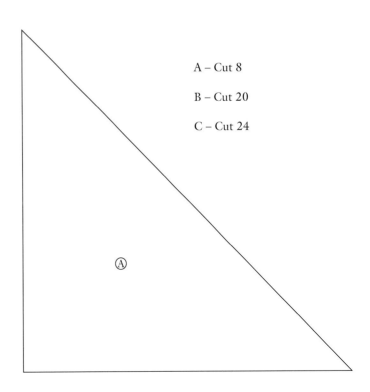

A – Cut 8

B – Cut 20

C – Cut 24

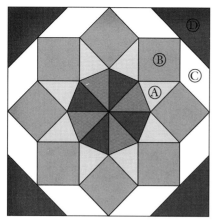

Kansas Dust Storm

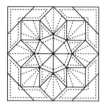

Quilting Ideas

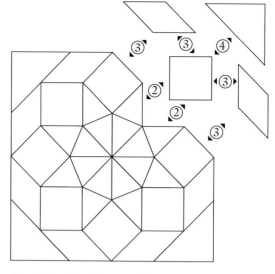

Step 1: Sew triangle shapes to form diamonds.

Step 2: Set in all squares.

Step 3: Set in the corner diamonds.

Step 4: Sew large triangles to the corners.

A – Cut 16

B – Cut 8

C – Cut 8

D – Cut 4

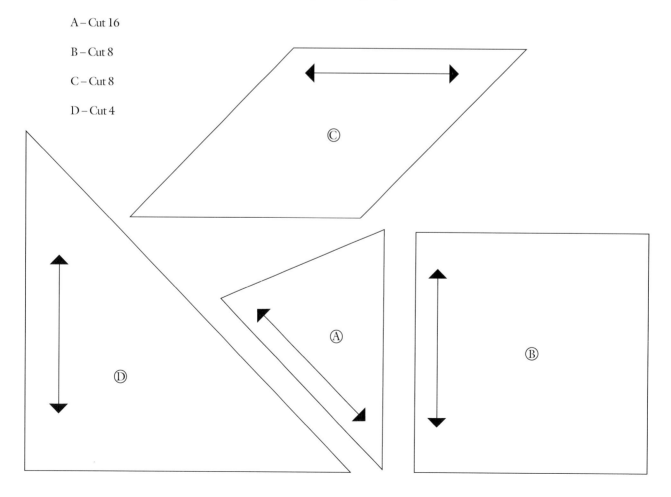

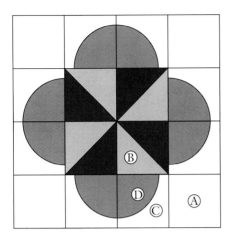

Curves and Straight

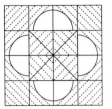 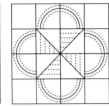

Quilting Ideas

A – Cut 4

B – Cut 8

C – Cut 8

D – Cut 8

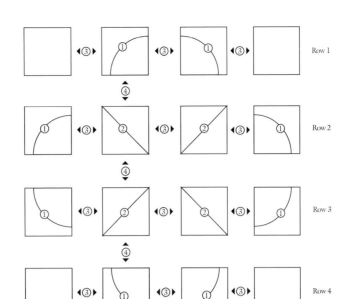

Row 1

Row 2

Row 3

Row 4

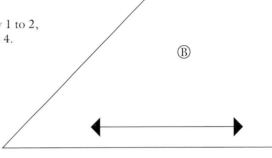

Step 1: Piece curves.

Step 2: Sew triangle squares.

Step 3: Sew rows.

Step 4: Sew row 1 to 2,
2 to 3, and 3 to 4.

Ⓑ

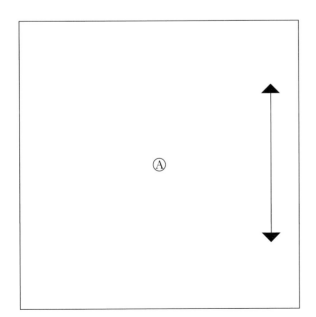

Ⓐ

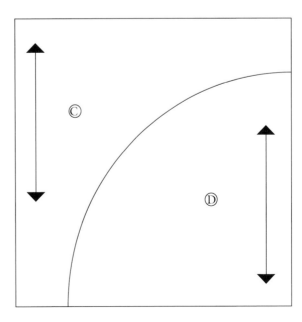

Ⓒ

Ⓓ

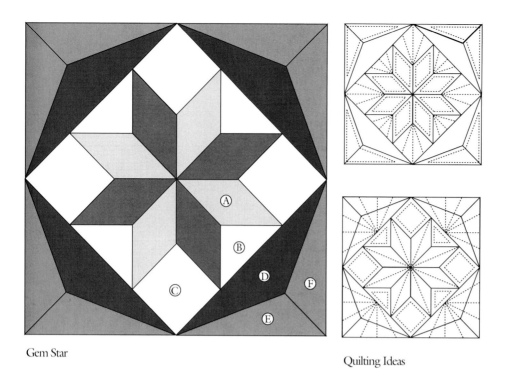

Gem Star

Quilting Ideas

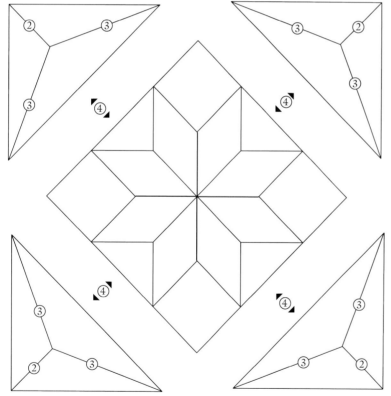

Step 1: Follow instructions in Lesson 7 for the center Eight Pointed Star section.

Step 2: Sew two outside corner pieces together.

Step 3: Set in the corner triangle.

Step 4: Sew the corner section to the center square.

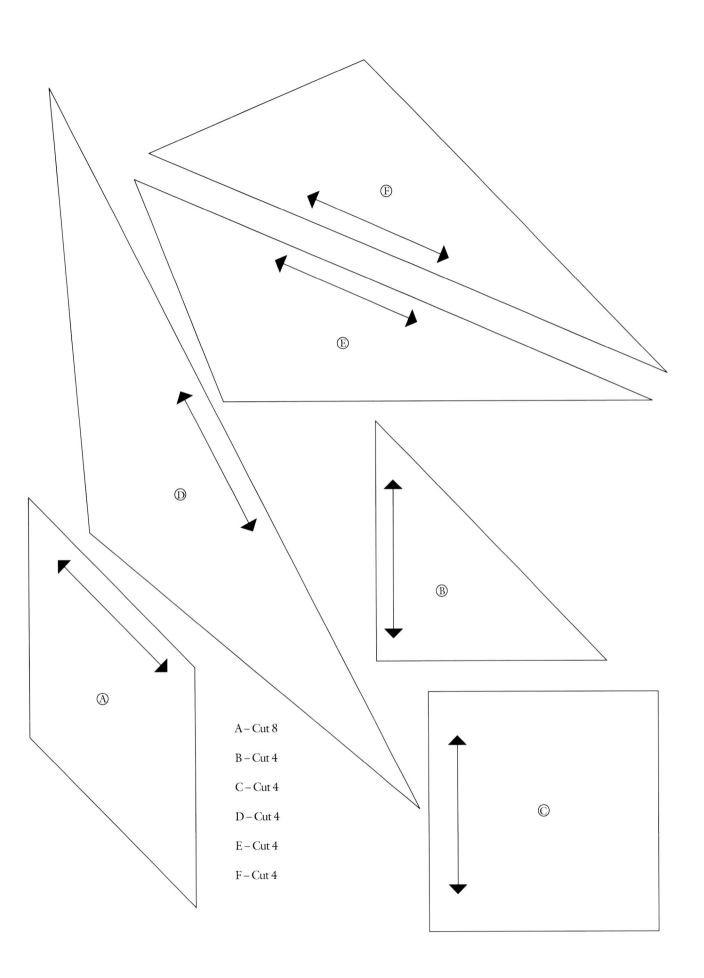

A – Cut 8

B – Cut 4

C – Cut 4

D – Cut 4

E – Cut 4

F – Cut 4

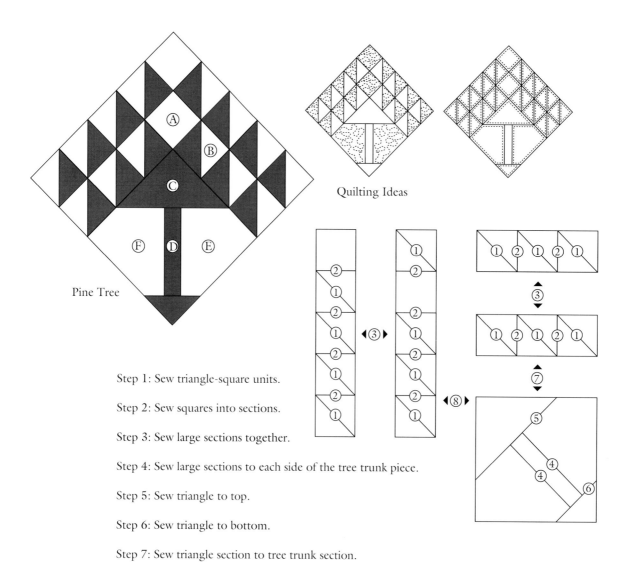

Pine Tree

Quilting Ideas

Step 1: Sew triangle-square units.

Step 2: Sew squares into sections.

Step 3: Sew large sections together.

Step 4: Sew large sections to each side of the tree trunk piece.

Step 5: Sew triangle to top.

Step 6: Sew triangle to bottom.

Step 7: Sew triangle section to tree trunk section.

Step 8: Sew step 7 to step 3 section.

A – Cut 2

B – Cut 29

C – Cut 1

D – Cut 1

E – Cut 1

F – Cut 1

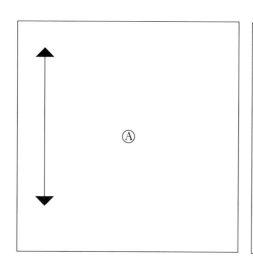

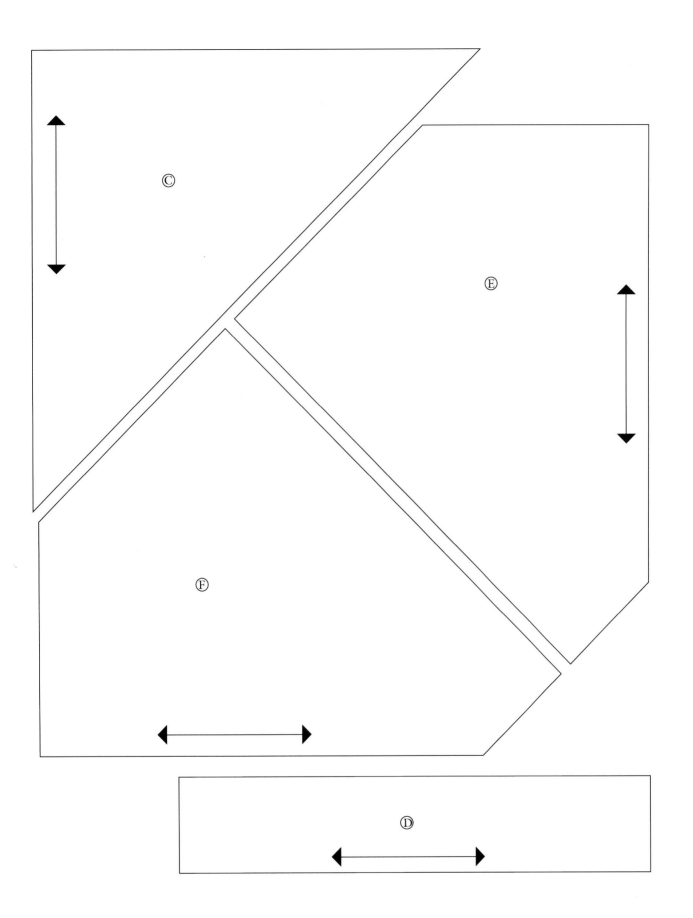

129

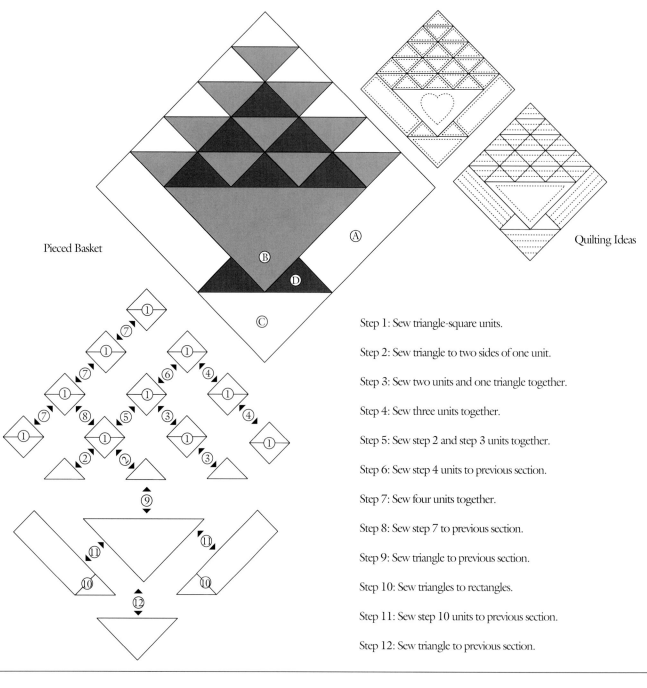

Pieced Basket

Quilting Ideas

Step 1: Sew triangle-square units.

Step 2: Sew triangle to two sides of one unit.

Step 3: Sew two units and one triangle together.

Step 4: Sew three units together.

Step 5: Sew step 2 and step 3 units together.

Step 6: Sew step 4 units to previous section.

Step 7: Sew four units together.

Step 8: Sew step 7 to previous section.

Step 9: Sew triangle to previous section.

Step 10: Sew triangles to rectangles.

Step 11: Sew step 10 units to previous section.

Step 12: Sew triangle to previous section.

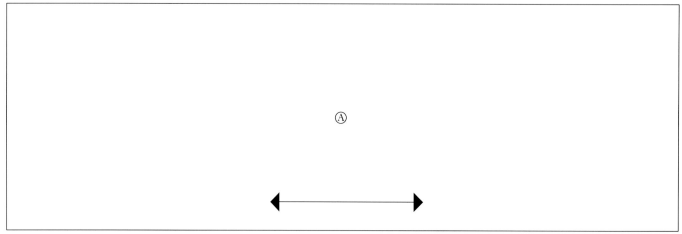

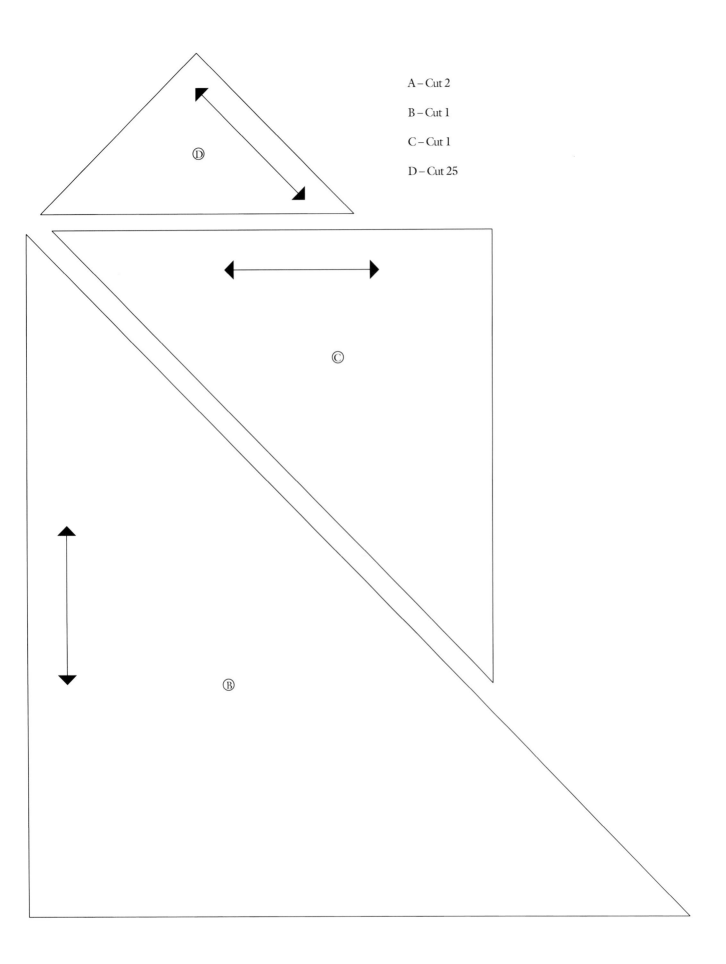

A – Cut 2

B – Cut 1

C – Cut 1

D – Cut 25

Ⓓ

Ⓒ

Ⓑ

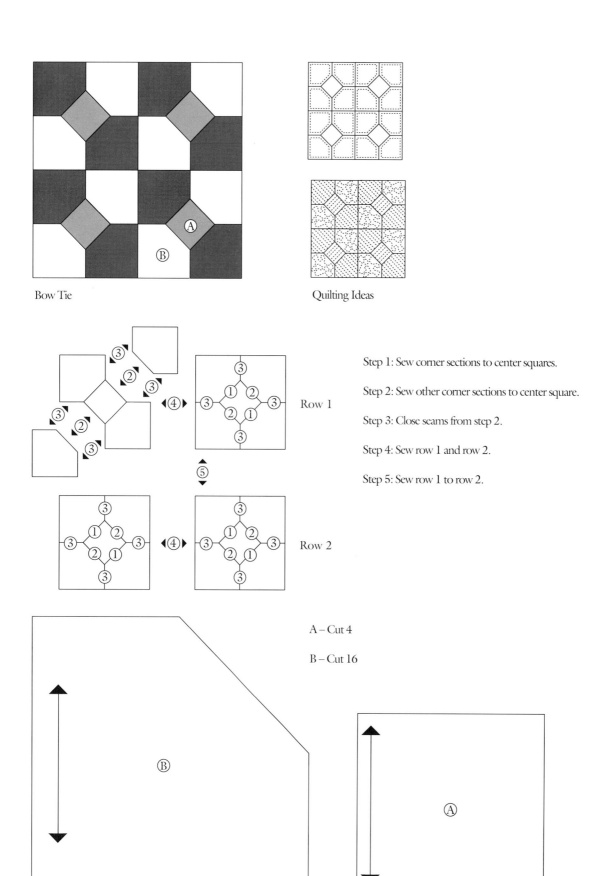

Bow Tie

Quilting Ideas

Row 1

Row 2

Step 1: Sew corner sections to center squares.

Step 2: Sew other corner sections to center square.

Step 3: Close seams from step 2.

Step 4: Sew row 1 and row 2.

Step 5: Sew row 1 to row 2.

A – Cut 4

B – Cut 16

Hawaiian Design

Quilting Ideas

Follow the directions in
Lesson 5 for the applique
of this block.

A – Cut 1 with fabric
folded so four layers are cut
at once.

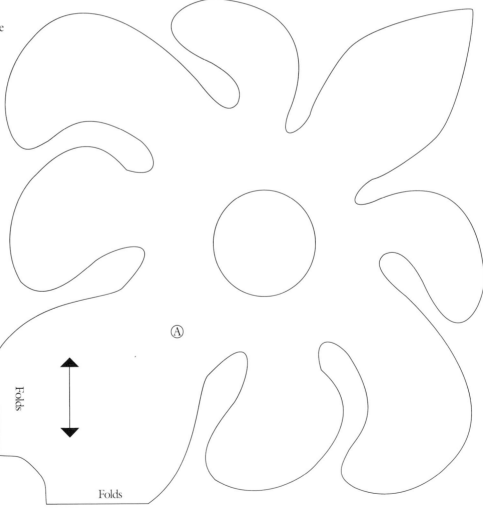

Folds

Ⓐ

Folds

133

Lancaster Rose

Quilting Ideas

Step 1: Applique leaves in place.

Step 2: Applique large petals.

Step 3: Applique small petals.

Step 4: Applique large center circle.

Step 5: Applique small center circle.

A – Cut 4

B – Cut 4

C – Cut 4

D – Cut 1

E – Cut 1

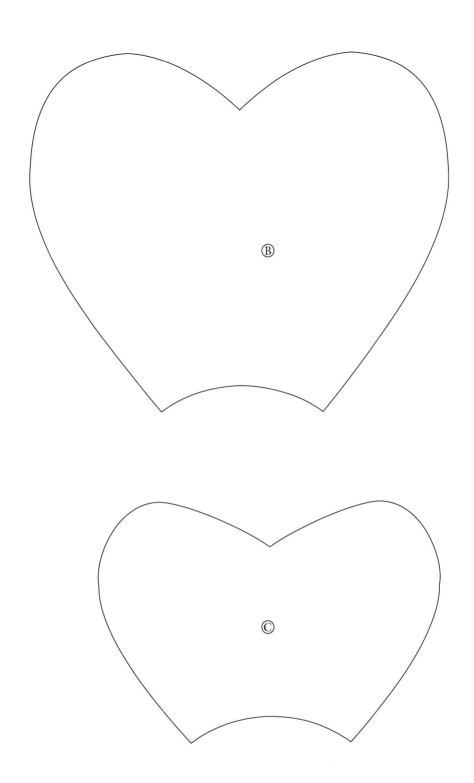

Ⓑ

Ⓒ

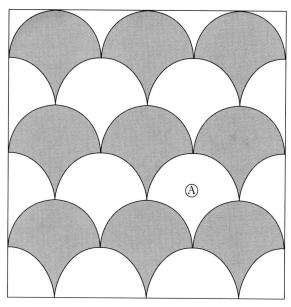

Clamshell

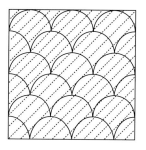 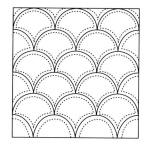

Quilting Ideas

Step 1: Cut a 12½" x 12½" square of muslin. The Clamshells are appliqued to the muslin square. Mark the muslin square with 2" lines in the horizontal direction only. The lines should start and stop ¼" from the top and bottom.

Step 2: Cut 25 Clamshell pieces.

Step 3: Start on the top row and work toward the bottom. The top Clamshells will sit with their sides on the 2" line and the bottom raw edge on the 4" line. At the very top you will need to insert the bases of some Clamshells to fill the background area.

A – Cut 25

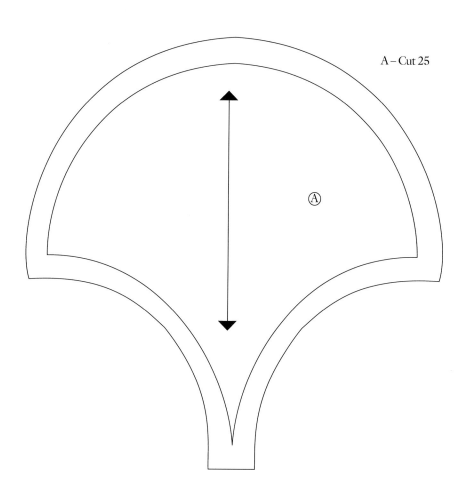

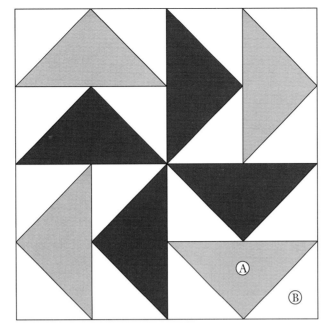

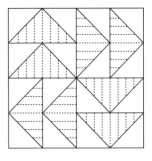

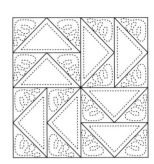

Dutchman's Puzzle

Quilting Ideas

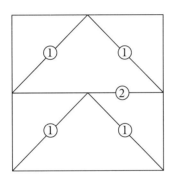

Step 1: Sew small triangles to each side of the large triangles.

Step 2: Sew the two shapes from step 1 together.

Step 3: Sew 4 squares that look like this.

Step 4: Sew 2 of the squares together to make row 1 and row 2.

Step 5: Sew row 1 to row 2.

A – Cut 8

B – Cut 16

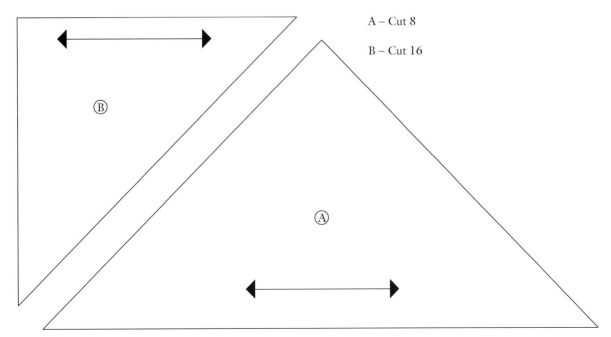

137

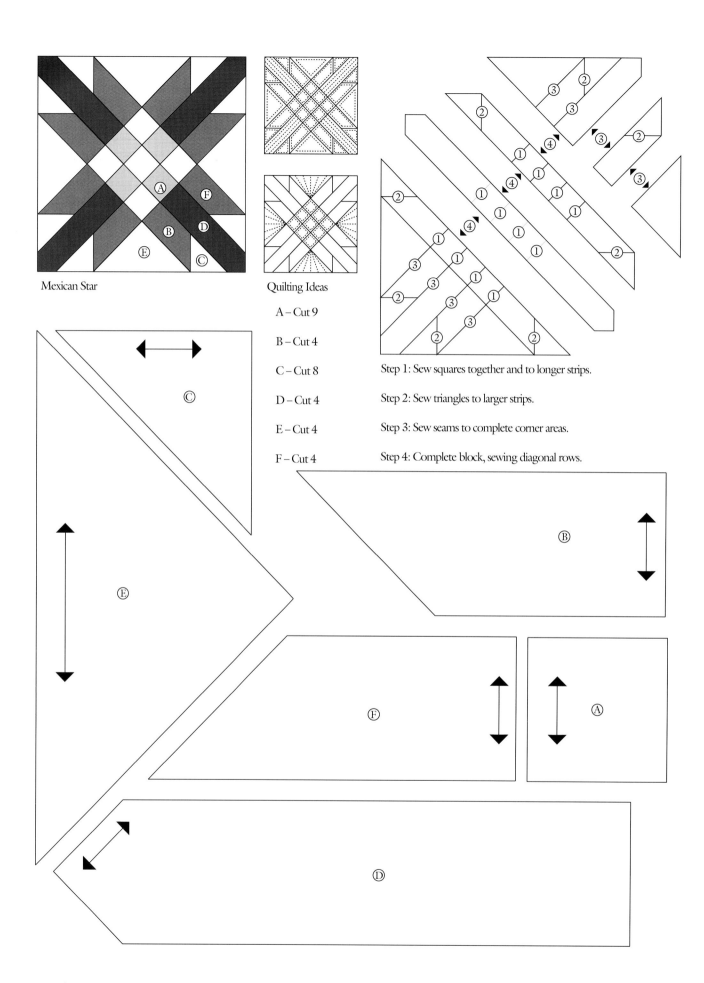

Mexican Star

Quilting Ideas

A – Cut 9

B – Cut 4

C – Cut 8

D – Cut 4

E – Cut 4

F – Cut 4

Step 1: Sew squares together and to longer strips.

Step 2: Sew triangles to larger strips.

Step 3: Sew seams to complete corner areas.

Step 4: Complete block, sewing diagonal rows.

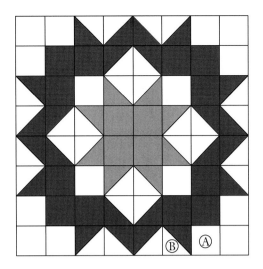
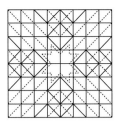
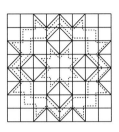

Carpenter's Wheel

Quilting Ideas

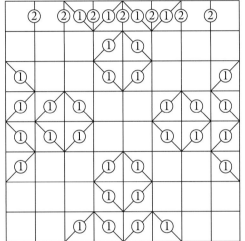
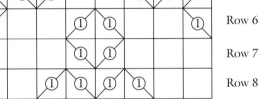
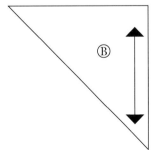

Row 1

Row 2

Row 3

Row 4

Row 5

Row 6

Row 7

Row 8

Step 1: Sew triangle-square units.

Step 2: Sew rows together.

Step 3: Sew row 1 to 2, 2 to 3, 3 to 4,
4 to 5, 5 to 6, 6 to 7, and 7 to 8.

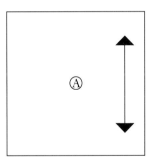

A – Cut 32

B – Cut 64

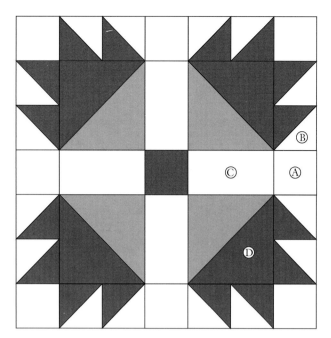

Bear's Paw

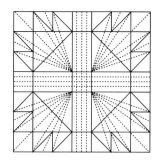

Quilting Ideas

Step 1: Sew triangle-square units.

Step 2: Sew triangle-square and square units together.

Step 3: Sew large triangle-squares.

Step 4: Sew small triangle-square rows to step 3.

Step 5: Sew longer triangle-square rows to step 4.

Step 6: Sew squares to rectangles.

Step 7: Sew step 5 to step 6.

Step 8: Sew step 7 units to long center strip.

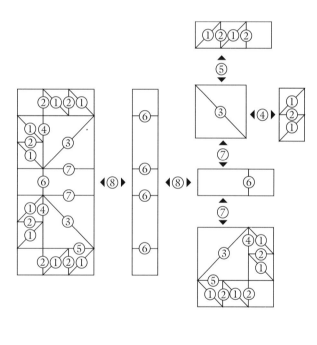

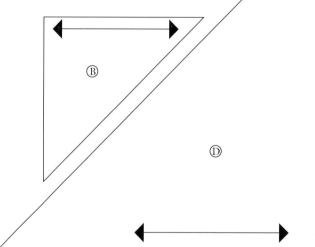

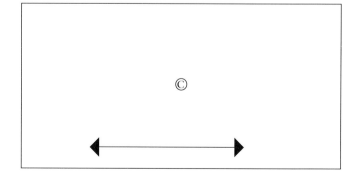

A – Cut 9

B – Cut 32

C – Cut 4

D – Cut 8

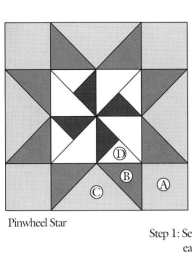

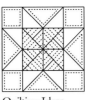 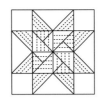

Quilting Ideas

Pinwheel Star

Step 1: Sew a small triangle to
each side of the large triangle.

Step 2: Sew two small triangles together.

Step 3: Sew a large triangle to step 5.

A – Cut 4

Step 4: Sew pieced squares together.

B – Cut 12

Step 5: Sew step 4 units together.

C – Cut 4

Step 6: Sew rows.

D – Cut 8

Step 7: Sew row 1 to 2, and row 2 to 3.

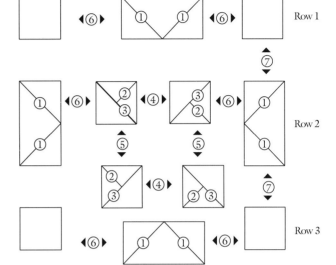

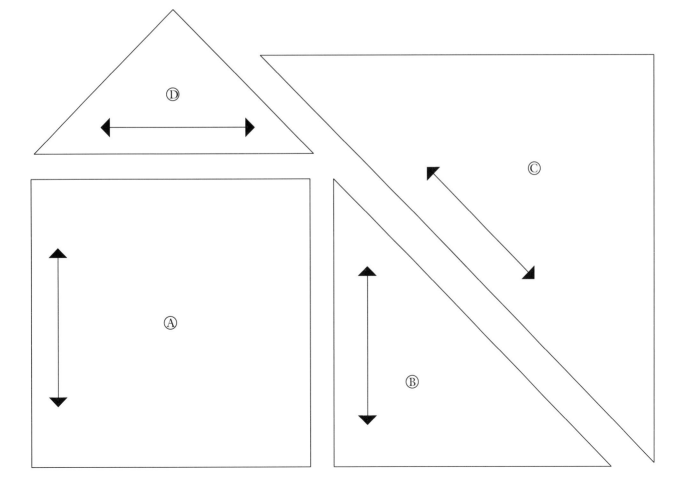

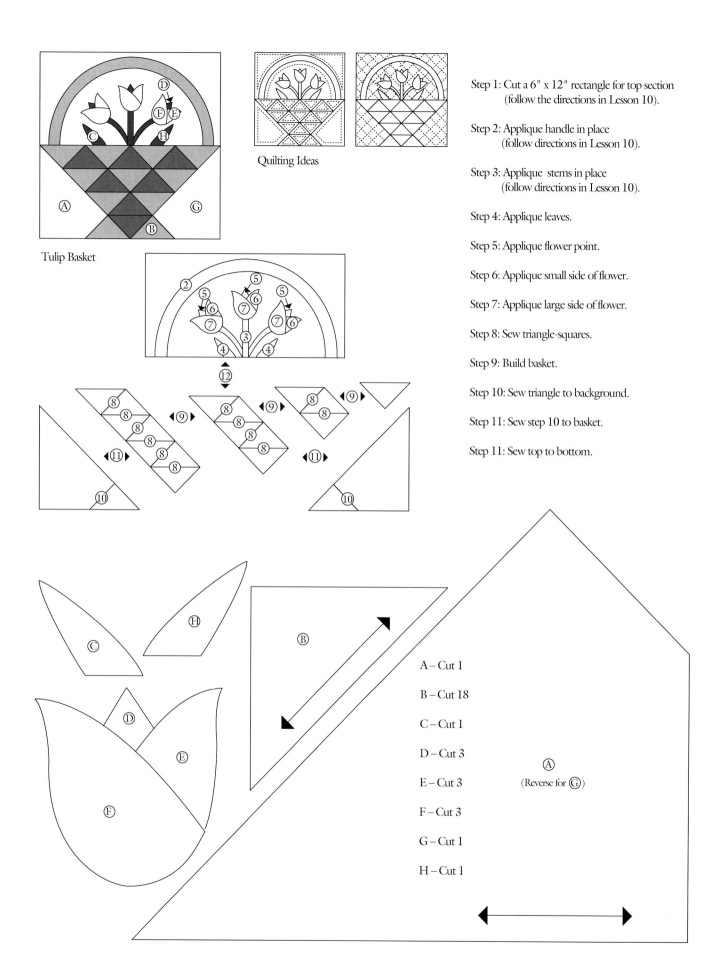

Tulip Basket

Quilting Ideas

Step 1: Cut a 6" x 12" rectangle for top section
(follow the directions in Lesson 10).

Step 2: Applique handle in place
(follow directions in Lesson 10).

Step 3: Applique stems in place
(follow directions in Lesson 10).

Step 4: Applique leaves.

Step 5: Applique flower point.

Step 6: Applique small side of flower.

Step 7: Applique large side of flower.

Step 8: Sew triangle-squares.

Step 9: Build basket.

Step 10: Sew triangle to background.

Step 11: Sew step 10 to basket.

Step 11: Sew top to bottom.

A – Cut 1

B – Cut 18

C – Cut 1

D – Cut 3

E – Cut 3

F – Cut 3

G – Cut 1

H – Cut 1

Ⓐ
(Reverse for Ⓖ)

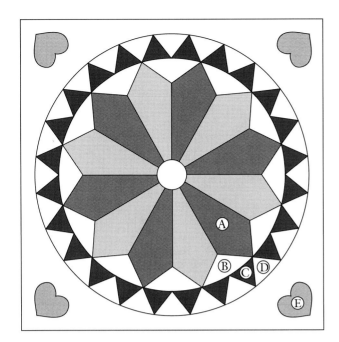

Dresden Wheel

Quilting Ideas

A – Cut 12

B – Cut 12

C – Cut 24

D – Cut 24

E – Cut 24

Step 1: Sew A pieces together to form circle.

Step 2: Set-in B pieces.

Step 3: Sew C pieces to D pieces until the circle is complete.

Step 4: Sew step 3 to step 2.

Step 5: Applique previous section to 12" background square.

Step 6: Applique a heart in each corner.

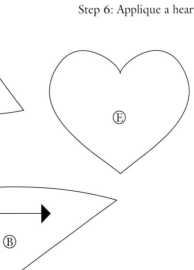

143

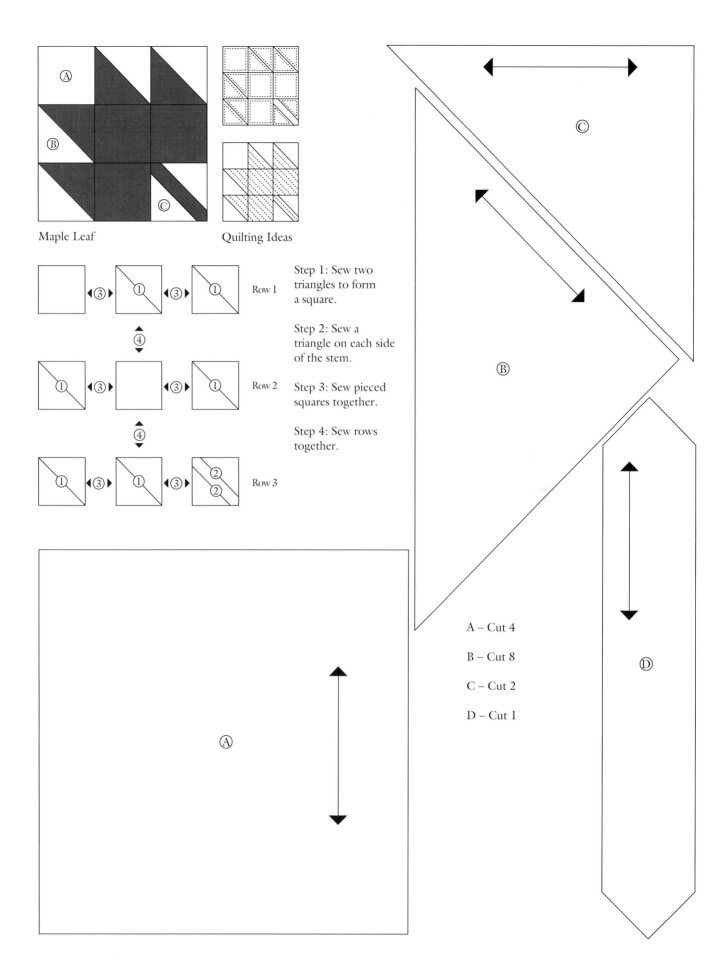

Maple Leaf

Quilting Ideas

Step 1: Sew two triangles to form a square.

Step 2: Sew a triangle on each side of the stem.

Step 3: Sew pieced squares together.

Step 4: Sew rows together.

Row 1

Row 2

Row 3

Ⓐ

Ⓑ

Ⓒ

Ⓓ

A – Cut 4

B – Cut 8

C – Cut 2

D – Cut 1

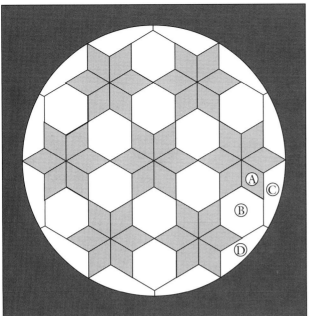

Seven Sisters

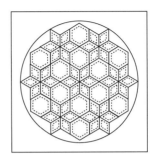

Quilting Ideas

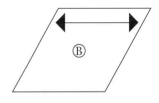

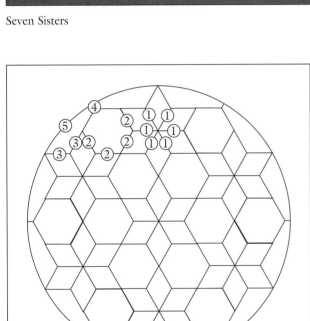

Step 1: Sew star shapes together.

Step 2: Set in hexagons as diagram shows.

Step 3: Set in outside shapes as diagram shows.

Step 4: Close seams at step 3.

Step 5: Applique design on to a 12" background square.

A – Cut 42

B – Cut 12

C – Cut 6

D – Cut 6

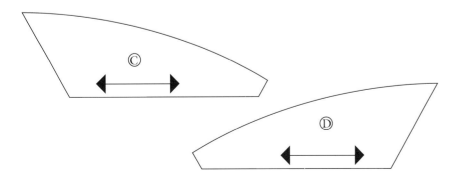

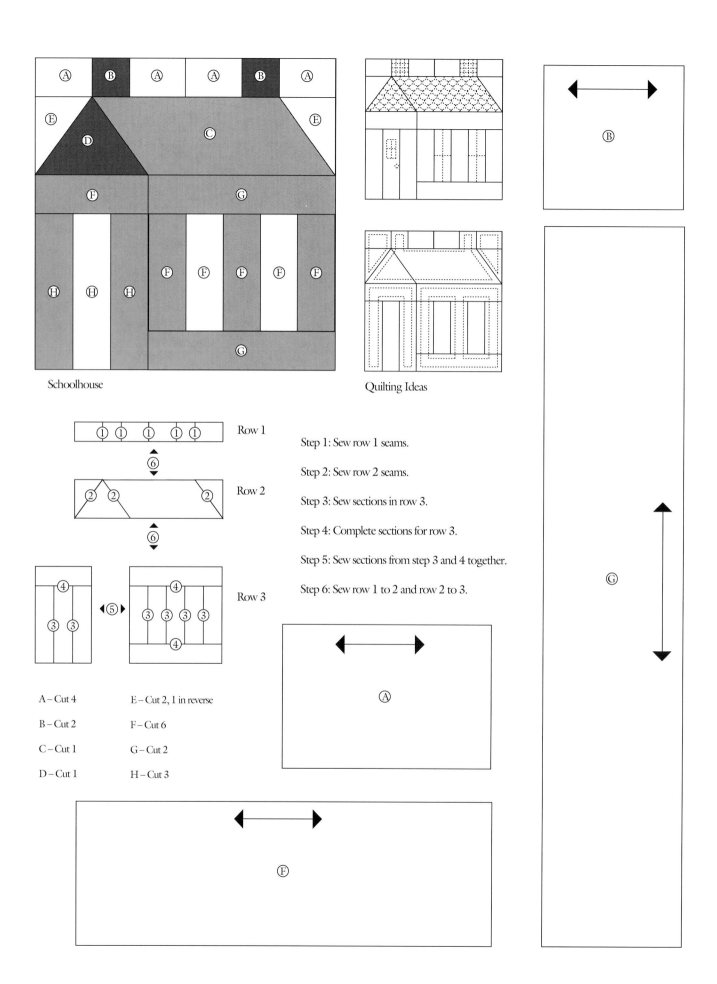

Schoolhouse

Quilting Ideas

Row 1

Row 2

Row 3

Step 1: Sew row 1 seams.

Step 2: Sew row 2 seams.

Step 3: Sew sections in row 3.

Step 4: Complete sections for row 3.

Step 5: Sew sections from step 3 and 4 together.

Step 6: Sew row 1 to 2 and row 2 to 3.

A – Cut 4         E – Cut 2, 1 in reverse

B – Cut 2         F – Cut 6

C – Cut 1         G – Cut 2

D – Cut 1         H – Cut 3

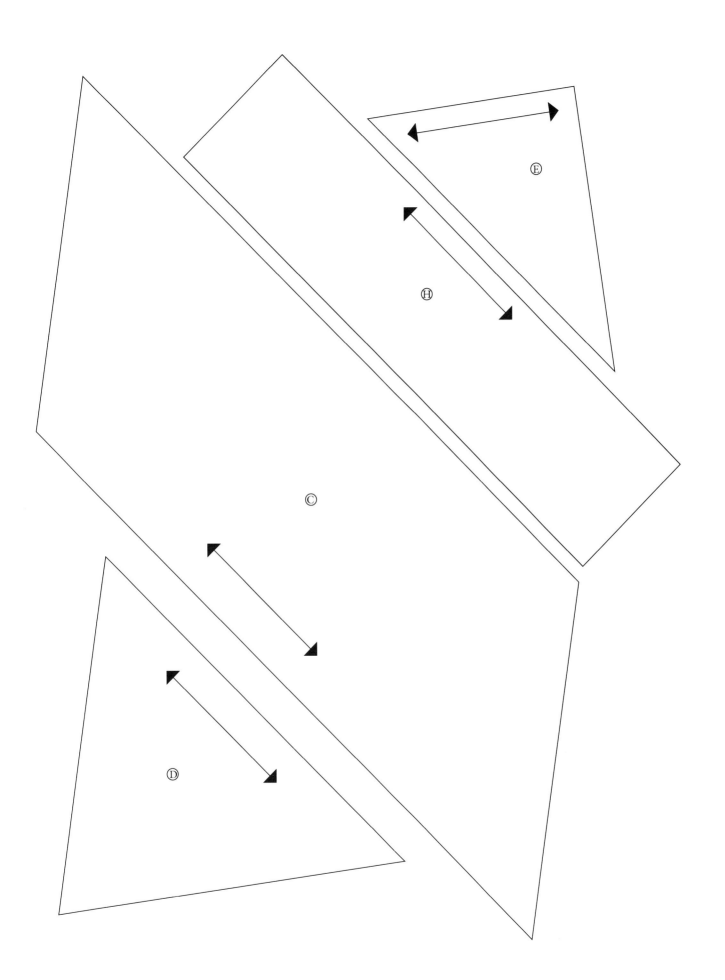

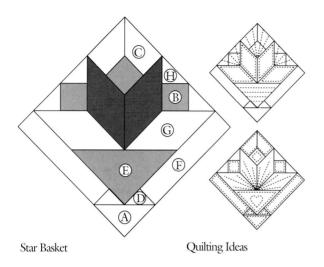

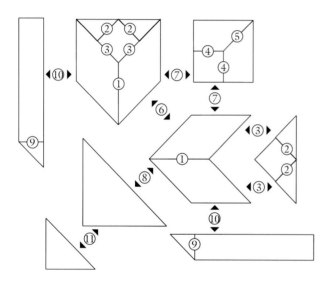

Star Basket          Quilting Ideas

Step 1: Sew 2 diamond shapes together.

Step 2: Sew a triangle to each side of a square.

Step 3: Set step 2 into step 1.

Step 4: Sew corner section to square.

Step 5: Close corner seam.

Step 6: Connect diamonds.

Step 7: Set-in corner section.

Step 8: Connect large triangle to previous steps.

Step 9: Sew small triangle to rectangle.

Step 10: Sew step 9 to previous section.

Step 11: Sew bottom triangle to previous section.

A – Cut 1

B – Cut 3

C – Cut 2, 1 in reverse

D – Cut 2

E – Cut 1

F – Cut 2

G – Cut 4

H – Cut 4

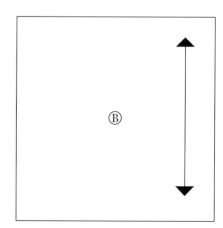

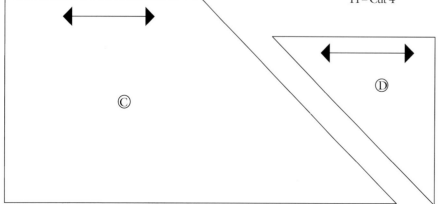

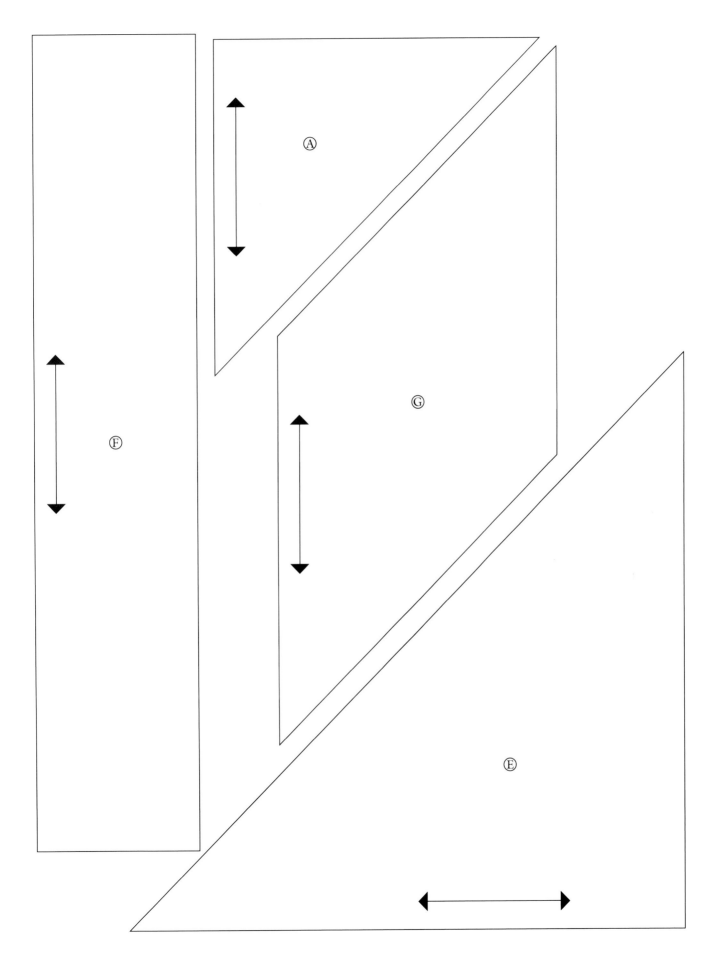

Ⓐ

Ⓕ

Ⓖ

Ⓔ

149

*The author, Karen Kay Buckley.*

Born and raised by the banks of the Susquehanna River in Halifax, Pennsylvania, Karen Kay Buckley graduated from Lock Haven University with a B.A. in teaching. She has been quilting for over ten years and has taught over a thousand men and women the art of quilting. She owned and operated a successful quilt shop in Bucks County, which continues to grow and prosper. She, her husband, Joe, and their dog, Samantha, currently reside outside of Carlisle, Pennsylvania, in a wonderfully restored federal-style farmhouse. The entire third floor of their home is devoted to Karen's studio. When not taking art or quilt classes or working with the local quilt club, Karen devotes her time to designing, lecturing and teaching that which gives her the greatest joy – quilting. She wants to hear from you if you have any questions. You can write to her at 1237 Holly Pike, Carlisle, PA 17013.

# Section FIVE

## Sampler Quilts

MEDALLION SAMPLER by Karen Buckley.

*SAMPLER QUILT by Sharyn Koenig.*

FLO'S QUILT, *pieced by Joe Buckley and quilted by Helen Hechert.*

*Above: SAMPLER QUILT by Karen Buckley.*

*Opposite Page:*
*Top left: SAMPLER QUILT by Karen Buckley.*
*Top right: A SAMPLER FOR SCOTT by Joan Amey.*
*Bottom: SAMPLER QUILT by Kyoko Fujimoto.*

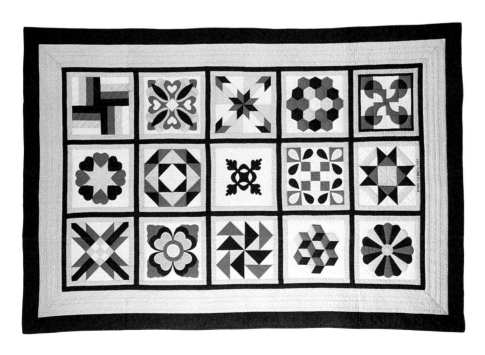

*Above: SAMPLER QUILT by Anne Soriero.*

*Opposite page:*
*Top left: BOBBY'S QUILT by Rosanne Zajko.*
*Top right: SAMPLER QUILT by Peg Buccilli.*
*Bottom: SAMPLER QUILT by Kathy King.*

*Above: PILLOWS by Dorrie Sillman, FRAMED BLOCK by Ruth Huzar and STUFFED BEAR by Linda Price.*

*Opposite page:*
*Top left: SAMPLER QUILT by Mary Jane Allen.*
*Top right: ANDREW'S QUILT by Sandy Focht.*
*Bottom: SAMPLER QUILT by Gale Adams.*

159

# American Quilter's Society
## dedicated to publishing books for today's quilters

*The following AQS publications are currently available:*

- **American Beauties: Rose & Tulip Quilts,** Gwen Marston & Joe Cunningham, #1907: AQS, 1988, 96 pages, softbound, $14.95
- **America's Pictorial Quilts,** Caron L. Mosey, #1662: AQS, 1985, 112 pages, hardbound, $19.95
- **Applique Designs: My Mother Taught Me to Sew,** Faye Anderson, #2121: AQS, 1990, 80 pages, softbound, $12.95
- **Arkansas Quilts: Arkansas Warmth,** Arkansas Quilter's Guild, Inc., #1908: AQS, 1987, 144 pages, hardbound, $24.95
- **The Art of Hand Applique,** Laura Lee Fritz, #2122: AQS, 1990, 80 pages, softbound, $14.95
- **...Ask Helen More About Quilting Designs,** Helen Squire, #2099: AQS, 1990, 54 pages, 17 x 11, spiral-bound, $14.95
- **Award-Winning Quilts & Their Makers: The Best of AQS Shows – 1985-1987,** edited by Victoria Faoro, #2207: AQS, 1991, 232 pages, soft bound, $19.95
- **Classic Basket Quilts,** Elizabeth Porter & Marianne Fons, #2208: AQS, 1991, 128 pages, softbound, $16.95
- **A Collection of Favorite Quilts,** Judy Florence, #2119 AQS, 1990, 136 pages, softbound, $18.95
- **Dear Helen, Can You Tell Me?...all about quilting designs,** Helen Squire, #1820: AQS, 1987, 56 pages, 17 x 11, spiral-bound, $12.95
- **Dyeing & Overdyeing of Cotton Fabrics,** Judy Mercer Tescher, #2030: AQS, 1990, 54 pages, softbound, $9.95
- **Flavor Quilts for Kids to Make: Complete Instructions for Teaching Children to Dye, Decorate & Sew Quilts,** Jennifer Amor #2356, AQS, 1991, 120 pages., softbound, $12.95
- **Fun & Fancy Machine Quiltmaking,** Lois Smith, #1982: AQS, 1989, 144 pages, softbound, $19.95
- **Gallery of American Quilts: 1849-1988,** #1938: AQS, 1988, 128 pages, softbound, $19.95
- **Gallery of American Quilts 1860-1989: Book II,** #2129: AQS, 1990, 128 pages, softbound, $19.95
- **The Grand Finale: A Quilter's Guide to Finishing Projects,** Linda Denner, #1924: AQS, 1988, 96 pages, softbound, $14.95
- **Heirloom Miniatures,** Tina M. Gravatt, #2097: AQS, 1990, 64 pages, softbound, $9.95
- **Home Study Course in Quiltmaking,** Jeannie M. Spears, #2031: AQS, 1990, 240 pages, softbound, $19.95
- **Infinite Stars,** Gayle Bong, #2283: AQS, 1992, 72 pages, softbound, $12.95
- **The Ins and Outs: Perfecting the Quilting Stitch,** Patricia J. Morris, #2120: AQS, 1990, 96 pages, softbound, $9.95
- **Irish Chain Quilts: A Workbook of Irish Chains & Related Patterns,** Joyce B. Peaden, #1906: AQS, 1988, 96 pages, softbound, $14.95
- **Marbling Fabrics for Quilts: A Guide for Learning & Teaching,** Kathy Fawcett & Carol Shoaf, #2206: AQS, 1991, 72 pages, softbound, $12.95
- **Missouri Heritage Quilts,** Bettina Havig, #1718: AQS, 1986, 104 pages, softbound, $14.95
- **Nancy Crow: Quilts and Influences,** Nancy Crow, #1981: AQS, 1990, 256 pages, hardcover, $29.95
- **No Dragons on My Quilt,** Jean Ray Laury with Ritva Laury & Lizabeth Laury, #2153: AQS, 1990, 52 pages, hardcover, $12.95
- **Oklahoma Heritage Quilts,** Oklahoma Quilt Heritage Project #2032: AQS, 1990, 144 pages, softbound, $19.95
- **Quiltmaker's Guide: Basics & Beyond,** Carol Doak, #2284: AQS, 1992, 208 pages, softbound $19.95
- **QUILTS: The Permanent Collection – MAQS,** #2257: AQS, 1991, 100 pages, 10 x 6½, softbound, $9.95
- **Scarlet Ribbons: American Indian Technique for Today's Quilters,** Helen Kelley, #1819: AQS, 1987, 104 pages, softbound, $15.95
- **Sets & Borders,** Gwen Marston & Joe Cunningham, #1821: AQS, 1987, 104 pages, softbound, $14.95
- **Somewhere in Between: Quilts and Quilters of Illinois,** Rita Barrow Barber, #1790: AQS, 1986, 78 pages, softbound, $14.95
- **Stenciled Quilts for Christmas,** Marie Monteith Sturmer, #2098: AQS, 1990, 104 pages, softbound, $14.95
- **Texas Quilts – Texas Treasures,** Texas Heritage Quilt Society, #1760: AQS, 1986, 160 pages, hardbound, $24.95
- **A Treasury of Quilting Designs,** Linda Goodmon Emery, #2029: AQS, 1990, 80 pages, 14 x 11, spiral-bound, $14.95
- **Wonderful Wearables: A Celebration of Creative Clothing,** Virginia Avery, #2286: AQS, 1991, 168 pages, softbound, $24.95

*These books can be found in local bookstores and quilt shops. If you are unable to locate a title in your area, you can order by mail from AQS, P.O. Box 3290, Paducah, KY 42002-3290. Please add $1 for the first book and 40¢ for each additional one to cover postage and handling.*